KARYMSKY VOLCANO
ERUPTING ON THE
KAMCHATKA
PENINSULA, RUSSIA

SOME KINDS OF LAVA CAN BE AS HOT AS 1165°F (629°C).

Absolute Expert

VOLCANOES

All the
LATEST
FACTS From
the Field

Lela Nargi
With National Geographic Explorer
Arianna Soldati

NATIONAL GEOGRAPHIC
Washington, D.C.

CONTENTS

CHAPTER 1

Volcanoes Here, There, Everywhere! 8

CHAPTER 2

Volcano Basics 34

AL VOLCAN
TO THE VOLCANO

CHAPTER 3

Living With Volcanoes 58

CHAPTER 4

Serious Science 84

Greetings from YELLOWSTONE National Park

ARIANNA SOLDATI

FOREWORD

'**ve always been a really curious person.** From an early age, I knew volcano science was going to be my thing. I remember exactly what happened to get me interested in volcanoes. In 1991, when I was about two years old, Mount Pinatubo in the Philippines erupted. I was thousands of miles away, in Milan, Italy, at the house I grew up in. But my parents were watching the news, and the television was showing footage of the eruption. It was explosive. There were mudflows, and a big ash cloud shot into the sky. Seeing a mountain blowing up like that made a huge impression on me. As my family will tell you, I didn't talk about anything else for weeks.

That was the first time I saw the power of a volcano, and I knew I didn't want it to be

ARIANNA STUDYING PITON DE LA FOURNAISE'S VOLCANIC SAND MADE OF THE MINERAL OLIVINE

my last! I wanted to learn as much as possible about them, and I talked about them nonstop. When I was a bit older, I always tried to get my parents to take me on vacation to a place where there was a volcano. I finally got my wish when I was 12 years old. That's when my parents agreed to take a trip to Mount Vesuvius near Pompeii, Italy. It wasn't erupting at the time, so I insisted that we climb it. The climb was hard for a city kid. The terrain got steeper with every step, and there was no shade where we could cool off. But the view was breathtaking: the first yellow spring flowers against the red volcanic terrain, with the blue Mediterranean Sea in the background.

When we got to the top, I looked down into the crater. It was deeper than I had imagined, with vertical crater walls. Only half of it was in sunlight, with the other in shade. The day before, I had visited the ancient city of Pompeii, which had been destroyed by Mount Vesuvius in A.D. 79. I couldn't help thinking how different the volcano must have looked back then. Now it was quiet. Yet I still felt the power of the place. I stayed on the crater rim, looking down inside the Earth, feeling very connected to our living planet. I was totally hooked.

Look for me throughout this book as we explore these incredible natural wonders. I can't wait to share my experiences with you!

—Arianna Soldati

STROMBOLI
ERUPTING INTO
THE NIGHT

CHAPTER 1

VOLCANOES HERE, THERE, EVERYWHERE!

WHEN I WAS A HIGH SCHOOL STUDENT, I WENT TO THE BIG ISLAND OF HAWAII

with some other international students. We were all excited about getting a break from the cold Montana winter, soaking up the sun, and swimming with turtles.

ARIANNA SOLDATI

But I was most looking forward to the day we were going to spend on Kīlauea, the biggest volcano in the world!

When that day came, we drove up the volcano and watched as the landscape transformed the farther we drove. By the time we reached the top, we were surrounded by black volcanic rocks as far as the eye could see. We looked down into the Halemaʻumaʻu crater. This ellipse-shaped pit is almost half a mile (almost 1 km) wide. Today there is a lava lake in the crater; but at the time I visited, there wasn't any visible lava. Too bad!

After checking out Halemaʻumaʻu, we drove on the famous "road to nowhere." It's been crossed by lava flows so many times, no one bothers to rebuild it anymore. As the day faded, we got out of the car and hiked with flashlights and headlamps across the cooled lava. We were headed to the spot where people from the volcano observatory had pointed telescopes toward Kīlauea's lava flow. The sky was very dark. The only bright spot was the glowing red lava flowing down a cliff and into the ocean. When the lava met the water, the lava immediately turned dark, and the water steamed at the point of contact. It was a highlight of the trip.

That same year, I traveled to another famous volcano, in Yellowstone National Park, Wyoming. It's not what you picture when you think about a volcano. There is no mountain, no active lava flow, and its crater is so big that you barely realize you are standing inside it. What you do see are geysers (springs that spew hot water and steam) and hot springs by the hundreds! These geothermal features indicate there's a magma source nearby. The geysers and hot springs are home to many colorful bacteria and algae, and some of the hot springs are as colorful as rainbows! Scientists think that life on Earth first formed in places just like Yellowstone.

These awe-inspiring experiences helped me see firsthand that volcanoes are amazing, active systems that are always changing.

KĪLAUEA'S HALEMA'UMA'U

THE ONLY BRIGHT SPOT WAS THE **GLOWING RED LAVA** FLOWING DOWN A CLIFF AND INTO THE OCEAN.

AL VOLCAN
TO THE VOLCANO

VISITORS CHECK OUT THE AMAZING COLORS OF THE GRAND PRISMATIC SPRING AT YELLOWSTONE NATIONAL PARK IN WYOMING.

VOLCANOES ARE DANGEROUS, DESTRUCTIVE, AND INCREDIBLY POWERFUL.

They can wipe out forests and whole cities, cause crops to fail and people to starve.

They can spew poisonous gas into the atmosphere and shoot out "bombs" of lava and rock. Their ash has cloaked parts of the planet in darkness for months at a time. Their magma—that's what you call hot liquid rock when it's still inside a volcano—can reach temperatures of 2120°F (1160°C). Their lava—that's what you call magma when it comes out of the Earth—can exceed temperatures of 1165°F (629°C). Lava can be ejected into the atmosphere with the same force as an exploding nuclear bomb. One volcano erupted so loudly, it ruptured the eardrums of sailors on a ship 40 miles (64.4 km) away!

Amazingly, though, volcanoes have also shaped our planet. They've formed seabeds under our oceans. They make our soils rich in nutrients so that we can grow healthy food to eat. They even help create our atmosphere through the release of gases. Yes, volcanoes are vital to creating and re-creating Earth as we know it. But our planet is not the only spot in our solar system that's home to volcanoes.

The Extraterrestrials—Volcanoes in Space

Volcanoes are not only responsible for shaping our planet. They're also responsible for how other bodies in our solar system have developed over millions and billions of years. In fact, scientists have discovered volcanoes on most of our system's planets, and even a few of their moons. Some of these volcanoes have long been extinct. Others are still active. Scientists also think they've found the first evidence of volcanic activity on an exoplanet, or planet outside our solar system. It's called 55 Cancri e and is located 40 light-years from Earth. The more we study space, the more

KĪLAUEA'S LAVA FLOWING INTO THE OCEAN

amazing things we're likely to learn about volcanoes not only close to home but also across the entire universe!

The first non-Earth body studied by scientists, though, was our moon. Astronomers have been looking up at it for thousands of years—with their bare eyes, then simple early telescopes. Now sophisticated equipment lets them explore the moon's unique features from here on Earth, 239,000 miles (384,633 km) away. Astronauts were able to get their first in-person view from the moon's surface when the National Aeronautics and Space Administration (NASA) sent them on Apollo space missions in the 1960s and 1970s.

When astronauts Buzz Aldrin and Neil Armstrong touched down at the moon's Sea of Tranquility in 1969, they became the first people on the moon. And they weren't standing on an ancient seabed (as early astronomers had suggested); they were standing on a vast field of hardened lava. The astronauts brought rock samples back to Earth for examination. Scientists discovered that the samples were made up of a kind of igneous rock called basalt, just like the rock that makes up one of Earth's most common types of lava. It had been ejected onto the surface of the moon when its core was still partially molten.

On the moon, volcanic action, also called volcanism, was different than it is on Earth. Most volcanoes on the moon are found on only one side. Volcanoes on Earth are spread across the planet. In addition, many scientists believe that the moon's lower gas levels mean lava wouldn't have been able to forcefully explode out of its mantle as happens with some of the volcanoes on our home planet. Instead, they imagine it must have flowed or even glided out smoothly and easily, eventually filling in the moon's craters to create large, flat "seas" rather than forming tall mountains.

ASTRONAUT BUZZ ALDRIN WALKING ON THE SURFACE OF THE MOON, JULY 1969

APPLES DAMAGED BY VOLCANIC ASH FROM MOUNT ASO IN JAPAN

SCIENTISTS DISCOVERED THAT THE MOON'S SURFACE WAS MADE UP OF AN IGNEOUS ROCK CALLED BASALT.

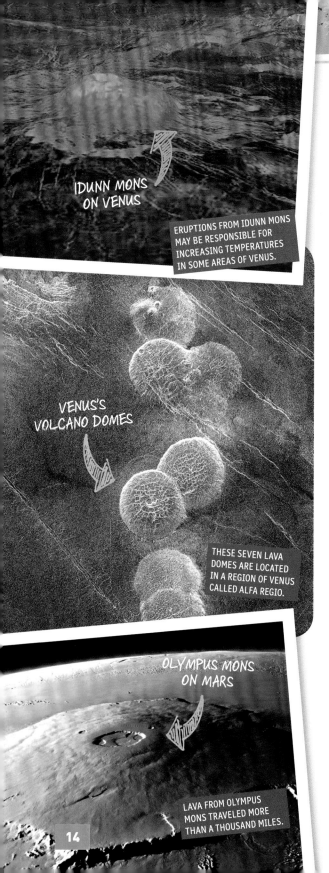

IDUNN MONS
ON VENUS

ERUPTIONS FROM IDUNN MONS MAY BE RESPONSIBLE FOR INCREASING TEMPERATURES IN SOME AREAS OF VENUS.

VENUS'S
VOLCANO DOMES

THESE SEVEN LAVA DOMES ARE LOCATED IN A REGION OF VENUS CALLED ALFA REGIO.

OLYMPUS MONS
ON MARS

LAVA FROM OLYMPUS MONS TRAVELED MORE THAN A THOUSAND MILES.

New discoveries about the moon's volcanism are being made all the time. In 1971 scientists discovered 70 strange-looking lava patches on the moon's surface. They didn't look like other lava patches. After some study, in 2014 they concluded that the patches had been made by explosive volcanic eruptions about 100 million years ago. That may sound like ancient history, but it means that there had been volcanoes erupting on the moon a lot more recently than scientists originally thought.

Another new discovery happened in 2016, when researchers found that there are enormous lava tubes running under the surface of the moon. These tubes are channels that form beneath lava flows. The ones on the moon are left over from when lava flows hardened millions of years ago. Some of the tubes are a mile (1.6 km) wide and 60 miles (96.6 km) long!

Other planets are also home to amazing volcanoes. Venus has the most inactive volcanoes of any of the planets in our solar system. This planet may also be home to the highest number of active volcanoes. But Earthlings have never been able to actually see them erupt. That's because the atmosphere around Venus is filled with gas clouds, which makes it difficult for us to see its surface clearly. However, that gas is actually an important clue that there are volcanoes on this planet and that some of them may be active! Much of the gas surrounding Venus is made up of thick sulfur dioxide, which is emitted when volcanoes erupt.

There are other clues, too. For example, we know that about 90 percent of Venus's surface is made of basalt. This rock is the result of hardened lava from early volcanic flows. And it appears the lava was responsible for shaping large parts of the surface of the planet. We also know that while it's already really hot on Venus—about 880°F (471°C)—a spacecraft orbiting the planet measured even hotter hot spots. Scientists hypothesized that the raised temperatures in these spots were caused by five separate lava flows spewing from a volcano called Idunn Mons.

Like Venus, Mars has a lot of volcanoes. You've probably heard of its most famous one: Olympus Mons. It's enormous. At over 16 miles (25.7 km) high and 310 miles (499 km) across, this volcano is wider than the Grand Canyon.

Luckily, we'd never see a volcano that big here on Earth. That's because Mars does not have tectonic plates that shift, allowing magma to rise through different places at different times. So when magma erupted from Olympus Mons, likely starting multibillions of years ago, it erupted through one spot where it was able to flow out in a constant stream. Throughout billions of years, the lava hardened and built up a gradual slope to form the colossal volcano we see today.

Olympus Mons isn't the only giant volcano on Mars. In the same region, a volcano called Alba Mons once spewed lava that traveled 1,243 miles (2,000 km) in one direction and 1,864 miles (3,000 km) in another. Nearby, Arsia Mons stands twice as tall as Mount Everest, and its caldera—or crater-shaped dent at its top—is a whopping 69 miles (111 km) across.

VENUS IS LOADED WITH VOLCANOES.

LAVA FROM MARS'S VOLCANOES FLOWED IN A STEADY STREAM.

Scientists recently figured out that Arsia Mons stopped erupting about 50 million years ago. Still, researchers are really interested in Arsia Mons because they think heat from one of its eruptions could have melted glaciers on Mars, creating huge lakes of water. If this is the case, it's possible that these lakes could have stuck around long enough to be colonized by microbes or other living things. Every living thing we know of requires water in order to exist. So where there's water, there's the possibility of current, former, or future life. Volcanoes may help us prove the existence of life on Mars!

Scientists have all kinds of evidence that volcanoes may be erupting on other worlds, too. But they don't usually get to *see* those eruptions happening. Io is a rare exception. The first time anyone ever saw a volcano erupting somewhere other than Earth was in 1979. That's when the spaceship Voyager 1 passed within 2.6 million miles (4,184,294 km) of Jupiter's fifth moon. It took pictures of an incredible sight: eight volcanoes erupting on Io.

Since then scientists have spied Io's volcanoes spouting 300-mile (483-km)-high fountains of lava and sulfur. And they've discovered that this moon also has vents that spew frozen vapor and "volcanic snow." As it turns out, Io is the most actively volcanic world in our solar system, with more than 160 active volcanoes counted so far. While the surface has patches of frost, Io also has the hottest lava around, reaching temperatures of over 2780°F (1527°C). Scientists believe some of this lava is a lot like lavas on Earth—made up of basaltic rock. But they think some of it is also made of sulfur and sulfur dioxide, which make volcanic plumes that are shaped like umbrellas and leave red, black, and white ash all over Io's surface.

Researchers are still observing Io carefully. Using NASA's space probe Voyager 1, scientists have collected a lot of data and images of Io and other places in our universe. Now they are also able to view Io's surface using powerful telescopes on Earth's surface. That means these telescopes help researchers see 390 million miles (627,644,160 km) away! Data is gathered about Io from other spacecraft that pass by this moon, en route to study other parts of space, too. Thanks to their observations, scientists now think they understand why this moon is so volcanic. Io orbits Jupiter, which has an intense gravitational pull. Jupiter's pull is so strong that it creates massive friction inside Io. That friction is strong enough to heat Io's interior until it's super hot and melted. The energy created from this friction and heat is so strong that it causes Io's volcanoes to erupt into space.

In fact, Io is so eruptive that scientists have been able to observe significant changes made to its surface. When spacecraft pass by Io and snap photos, scientists can see how much lava its volcanoes have ejected since the last pictures were taken.

IO HAS THE HOTTEST LAVA AROUND.

VOYAGER 1 IMAGE OF IO'S VOLCANIC PLAINS

LOKI PATERA, AN ACTIVE LAVA LAKE

The Submarines—Volcanoes Beneath the Waves!

Back here on Earth, we have about 1,500 *active* volcanoes—that is, volcanoes scientists think could erupt at any time. Five hundred of them actually *have* erupted since people started keeping track of this information. But there are many more volcanoes in existence on our planet than people ever get to witness firsthand. That's because they're deep underwater. An estimated 80 percent of Earth's volcanoes erupt under the ocean, often completely undetected.

Underwater, lava flows slowly and cools quickly. Over time, this lava can build up enough that the volcano eventually pops its head out of the water, and voilà! An island is born. All the Hawaiian Islands were formed like this, and so were the Galápagos Islands and even Iceland. But amazingly, new islands are forming all the time. One of them showed up in Japan in 2013, in

ARTIST'S IMPRESSION OF WHAT A CRYOVOLCANO ERUPTION ON TRITON MIGHT LOOK LIKE

ICE VOLCANOES ERUPT A COLD SLUDGE— **CRYOMAGMA.** THIS IS MADE UP OF WATER AND SUBSTANCES LIKE METHANE AND AMMONIA.

TRITON AS SEEN BY NASA'S VOYAGER SPACECRAFT

WHAT'S A CRYOVOLCANO?

YOU KNOW SOME VOLCANOES SPEW HOT LAVA, but did you know there are some that spew ice? On Io's moons and other worlds, cryovolcanoes—*kryos* means "freezing" in Greek—dominate the landscape. Beyond Mars, at least five moons and dwarf planets (that's what scientists call a planet that's round and orbits the sun but does not have the gravitational power to pull in or push away other smaller bodies) have cryovolcanoes: Jupiter's moon Europa, Saturn's moons Enceladus and Titan, Neptune's moon Triton, and dwarf planets Ceres and Pluto.

Like regular volcanoes, ice volcanoes erupt because of built-up heat and pressure inside the planet, moon, or other celestial body they exist on.

Volcanoes that form on planets and moons that are rocky erupt lava made of molten rock. But ice volcanoes erupt a cold sludge—cryomagma. Cryomagma is made up of water and other substances such as methane and ammonia. Under a moon or planet's surface, these substances are warm and remain in either solid or liquid form. Eventually, they get hot enough to turn into gas. Then pressure builds, and the materials shoot out onto the frigid surface, where they instantly freeze.

LAVA CAN BUILD UP ENOUGH THAT THE VOLCANO EVENTUALLY POPS ITS HEAD OUT OF THE WATER, AND VOILÀ! AN ISLAND IS BORN.

NĀPALI COAST OF THE HAWAIIAN ISLAND OF KAUAI

MAPPING THE OCEAN FLOOR

ONE OF THE REASONS scientists know so little about underwater volcanoes is that they haven't been sure where to look for them. But that began to change in 2014, when researchers created a new, very detailed map of the entire ocean floor. Just like that, we went from thinking there are 5,000 submarine volcanoes to knowing there are at least 10,000 of them. And in the process, we discovered two huge volcanic ridges we hadn't known existed before. One is in the Gulf of Mexico and is as wide as the state of Texas. Another that's in the southern Atlantic Ocean is an incredible 500 miles (805 km) long. As of yet, none of the volcanoes in this range have erupted (that we know about!).

MAP OF THE ATLANTIC OCEAN FLOOR

ATLANTIC OCEAN

AFRICA

SOUTH AMERICA

the ocean south of Tokyo. Islands like these often are eroded by waves before birds and insects and trees (and humans!) have a chance to make their homes on them. But sometimes they stick around, and the world as we know it is changed forever.

Black Smokers

Above or below water, volcanoes are volcanoes, right? Nope! Take black smokers, also known as hydrothermal vents. These underwater features were first discovered in 1977 by a submersible (a craft that can operate completely underwater) studying the waters around the Galápagos Islands. Black smokers are created by cracks on the bottom of the sea. Instead of spewing lava, these cracks let frigid ocean water seep down beneath the Earth's crust. There, cold water meets fiery magma.

THE SUBMERSIBLE *ALVIN* HELPING SCIENTISTS STUDY THE DEEP OCEAN

The magma heats the water, which causes enough pressure to blast the water back up.

These hydrothermal plumes can reach temperatures of 700°F (371°C) and are mixed with minerals like sulfur, copper, gold, zinc, and iron that the water picks up as it moves along. When these minerals harden, they build up into narrow chimneys around the cracks.

Most black smokers are found deeper than a mile (1.6 km) underwater, near what are called the mid-ocean ridges, where two tectonic plates pull apart from each other. They are important for maintaining life in places where it's otherwise too dark for organisms to grow. Without the light of the sun, there's no photosynthesis to make the energy that plants "eat." But the sulfur and other minerals and chemicals spewing out of these vents feed microbes in a process called chemosynthesis: The microbes eat the sulfur

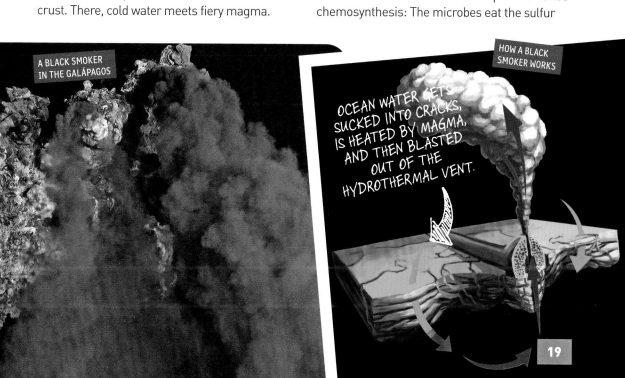

A BLACK SMOKER IN THE GALÁPAGOS

HOW A BLACK SMOKER WORKS

OCEAN WATER GETS SUCKED INTO CRACKS, IS HEATED BY MAGMA, AND THEN BLASTED OUT OF THE HYDROTHERMAL VENT.

19

CREATURES OF THE BLACK SMOKERS

DEEP-SEA URCHINS GROWING ON LAVA NEAR NEW ZEALAND

ORGANISMS THAT LIVE IN EXTREME environments are called extremophiles. The thousands of kinds of extremophiles that live around black smokers have some pretty awesome abilities. Here are just a few.

Methanopyrus kandleri is a tiny organism. It loves salt and heat, and it can survive in temperatures up to 230°F (110°C). It makes its home on the superhot chimneys of black smokers. There it "eats" hydrogen and turns it into methane.

Desulfonauticus submarinus is a bacterium that lives in the guts of three-foot (1 m)-long Pompeii worms that live on the vents. The bacteria "eat" sulfur and turn it into other compounds that are then eaten by the worms.

Green sulfur bacteria are a family of teensy extremophiles. Like *Desulfonauticus submarinus*, they need sulfur to survive. But they also need light. And that's something that doesn't exist in underwater vents. So what's a green sulfur bacterium to do? Find another light source. They capture light from the radioactive glow that's emitted by volcanically heated rocks.

Other interesting creatures of the hot deep include little crustaceans called copepods, leeches, sponges, jellies, sea stars, eels, anemones, clams, and crabs. There's a lot of life to be found where you least expect it!

MUSSELS AND SHRIMP LIVING ON A HYDROTHERMAL VENT IN THE PACIFIC OCEAN

and produce other compounds that feed other life-forms. This process creates an ecosystem. The microbes form symbiotic relationships with other organisms—that is, a mutually beneficial arrangement in which the microbes get to set up house on a giant tube worm, for example, in exchange for making food for the tube worms.

Possibly the coolest thing of all about black smokers is that scientists think they might be where all of life on Earth started almost four billion years ago!

Axial Seamount

Just 300 miles (483 km) off the coast of Oregon, an undersea volcano half a mile (0.8 km) high,

SNOW IN HAWAII? FIND IT ON MAUNA KEA!

FROM ITS BASE ON THE OCEAN FLOOR TO ITS SUMMIT, MAUNA KEA IS TECHNICALLY THE TALLEST MOUNTAIN ON EARTH.

UP CLOSE WITH SEAMOUNTS

SEAMOUNTS ARE UNDERWATER MOUNTAINS. They usually rise from between 3,000 and 13,000 feet (914 and 3,962 m) off the ocean floor. Some of them even rise high enough to become islands—Hawaii's Mauna Kea started as a seamount (and it's also, technically, the highest mountain on the planet!). Seamounts take up a whole lot of room on the ocean floor. By some estimates, they occupy 18 million square miles (46,619,786 square km)—more than any other single kind of habitat on Earth. They're responsible for carrying nutrients up through the water from the bottom of the ocean. These nutrients feed corals, sea fans, fish, crustaceans, and many creatures that exist only around their very specialized ecosystems.

called the Axial Seamount, has done a lot to help us understand how to predict volcanic eruptions. It's the most active of the volcanoes on the Juan de Fuca ridge. A ridge is where two tectonic plates separate and let lava flow out.

When scientists started watching the Axial Seamount, they soon discovered that it had a lot of interesting behaviors. For starters, after it erupted in 2011, it didn't go right back to sleep. Instead, it instantly began puffing up like a balloon again. That's because the seafloor underneath it was starting to rise, which meant it was refilling with magma. Then, as another volcanic eruption approached, in April 2015 more than 2,000 earthquakes a day

MONITORING EQUIPMENT AT THE MOUTH OF AN AXIAL SEAMOUNT VENT

happened. When the eruption finally occurred on April 24, there were 600 earthquakes going off every hour!

When it blew, the Axial Seamount erupted lava out of at least two vents, one of which grew to be an incredible nine miles (14.5 km) long. By the time it was done erupting about a month later, it had pumped 79 billion gallons (300 billion L) of lava into the Pacific Ocean. This amazing event gave scientists a new understanding of the signs that lead up to a volcanic eruption. This information may one day help to better predict when explosions will happen at land-based volcanoes—and also help save lives in the process.

Greatest Hits: Earth's Most Amazing Volcanoes

All volcanoes can prove to be powerful forces. But they're not all created equal. Here are some volcano all-stars!

The Biggest

There are a few ways to determine the size of a volcano. One way is to measure how tall it is. In this category, Mauna Kea in Hawaii is the clear winner. Its summit is 13,797 feet (4,205 m) above sea level. But if you measure it from where it actually begins, under the Pacific Ocean, it's 33,500 feet (10,211 m) tall. That makes it not only the world's tallest volcano but also the world's tallest mountain—taller even than Mount Everest in Nepal's Himalaya mountains, which is 29,035 feet (8,850 m) from bottom to top. Mauna Kea is still considered *active* even though it last erupted about 4,500 years ago. That's because there's still magma beneath it, which means it likely won't stay asleep forever.

The biggest volcano in terms of how much space it takes up on land—also known as its footprint—is Tamu Massif, located about 1,000 miles (1,609 km) off the coast of Japan. This extinct, bowl-shaped shield volcano covers an area of more than 100,000 square miles (258,999 sq km), which is bigger than the entire state of New Mexico. That's so much bigger than the world's largest *active* volcano: Hawaii's Mauna Loa, which covers an area of just 2,000 square miles (5,180 sq km). Tamu Massif put on its bulk starting about 145 million years ago. It was unknown to science for a long time, and once it was finally discovered in 1993, it was mistakenly thought to be three volcanoes instead of one enormous one. That's because, believe it or not, it's not easy to see. Tamu Massif actually sits 6,500 feet (1,981 m) under the Pacific Ocean.

The Most Powerful

Yellowstone is an amazing national park in the states of Wyoming, Montana, and Idaho. But it's also home to a supervolcano. Supervolcanoes are called "super" because they are thousands of times more powerful than a regular volcano.

Supervolcanoes are not shaped like mountains but usually appear as depressions in the earth. These depressions are called calderas, and they have huge magma chambers under the

MAUNA LOA, IN HAWAII, IS THE LARGEST ACTIVE VOLCANO ON EARTH.

Earth's crust. After they erupt, the ground over the now-semi-empty magma chamber collapses, creating a giant depression.

Yellowstone is actually made up of three calderas, which were created after massive eruptions 2.1 million years ago, 1.3 million years ago, and 640,000 years ago. Scientists think that if the magma chambers were to fill up and erupt again, the amount of ash they would spew would be so thick it would destroy crops all over the Midwest and pollute rivers and streams, killing fish and making the water undrinkable. A blast might also block out sunlight for more than 10 years, vastly changing our world.

Scientists report that there's no evidence that magma is building up beneath Yellowstone's calderas, and there are no eruptions predicted for anytime in the near future.

Unfortunately, scientists in 1600 could not predict that a small Peruvian volcano called Huaynaputina would be responsible for the largest volcanic eruption in South America and also one of the largest eruptions on Earth. Before it blew, Huaynaputina caused four days' worth of serious earthquakes. Once it erupted, it sent an ash plume almost 22 miles (35.5 km) into the sky. Ash fell for 11 days, covering 224,000 square miles (580,157 sq km) of land and burying people, animals, crops, and homes. The eruption set off deafening thunder and 40 hours of darkness. By the time it was over, it had destroyed several villages and two cities, killed untold numbers of villagers, and sent hot mud pouring into the ocean 75 miles (121 km) away.

Another huge eruption happened in 1883, when the island of Krakatau, in Indonesia, erupted with 13,000 times more force than was created by the nuclear bomb dropped on Hiroshima, Japan, during World War II. More than 36,000 people lost their lives. Many of those deaths were the result of the huge tsunamis—giant waves of water—that were set off by the eruption. In addition, a fast-moving, superhot surge of gas and rock traveled across water to an island some 24 miles (38.6 km) away.

1938 POSTER FOR YELLOWSTONE NATIONAL PARK

CASTLE GEYSER AT YELLOWSTONE

ANAK KRAKATAU ("CHILD OF KRAKATAU") VOLCANO, INDONESIA

NOVARUPTA'S CRATER IN THE VALLEY OF TEN THOUSAND SMOKES

The sound of the volcano exploding could be heard almost 3,000 miles (4,828 km) away. Spewed ash from the volcano traveled almost 3,800 miles (6,116 km), and temperatures dropped in the first year after the eruption and didn't climb back to normal for another four years. Even now, Krakatau is experiencing small eruptions, getting ready for another big bang, but no one knows when it might erupt again.

The biggest explosion of the 20th century happened in Alaska's Valley of Ten Thousand Smokes in June 1912. That's when a volcano called Novarupta exploded. Its lava was sucked out of a magma chamber lying inside Earth's crust six miles (9.7 km) away, beneath Mount Katmai. When Novarupta erupted, Mount Katmai promptly collapsed into a caldera two miles (3.2 km) wide. The blast was strong enough to be heard 750 miles (1,207 km) away, in the city of Juneau, and ash fell on Kodiak

Island, 100 miles (161 km) away, for three days. The ash also traveled on the wind all the way to Africa. Luckily, villagers near Novarupta had paid attention to the earthquakes in the days leading up to the blast, so most of them had evacuated before the volcano blew. Witnesses reported the sky turning pitch black, the water of a local bay churning to a white froth, air so thick with ash it was hard to breathe, and dead salmon floating in the rivers. Novarupta is one of the five strongest blasts in recorded history.

The Most Active

In the waters off the southern coast of Italy, where the Ionian, Mediterranean, and Tyrrhenian Seas meet, lies a feature known as the Calabrian Arc. This is where two tectonic plates come together, one under the other, to create two of the world's most active stratovolcanoes. One of these is Stromboli, and the other is Mount Etna.

Stromboli sits on Stromboli the island, off the coast of Sicily in Italy. The island was "built" by lava from volcanic eruptions that began 200,000 years ago. Stromboli has erupted off and on for the last 2,000 years, but almost nonstop since 1932. Sometimes it vents steam out of its top. And every 15 minutes or so, it blows huge fountains of lava high into the sky. These eruptions are so bright and can be seen from so far away that they've earned Stromboli the nickname "Lighthouse of the Mediterranean."

To the south of Stromboli, on the island of Sicily, Mount Etna has been erupting for almost 500,000 years! Its eruptions usually come out of vents near the summit of the 10,922-foot (3,320-m)-tall volcano. It's the biggest in Europe and one of the tallest on the planet. In the 1600s, lava from Etna changed the shape of the island's coastline. In the 1980s, its eruptions destroyed forests and vineyards. But the "Friendly Giant," as Etna is nicknamed, also provides its islanders with fertile soil that's good for planting crops. The volcano also attracts tons of visitors who fly in hoping for an up-close look at a blast.

Half a world away from Etna and Stromboli is Mount Yasur, a volcano that sits on Tanna Island, part of the tiny island nation of Vanuatu. Incredibly, Yasur has been erupting several times an hour for at least the last 800 years! This volcano has been known to Westerners since 1774. That's when British explorer Captain James Cook wrote in his ship's log about seeing a volcano that "threw up vast quantities of fire and smoke and made a rumbling noise which was heard at a great distance." Some of Yasur's eruptions send clouds of gas and ash 6,500 feet (1,981 m) into the air!

SEEN FROM ABOVE: STROMBOLI, OFF SICILY'S COAST

MOUNT ETNA SPEWS A COLUMN OF ASH AND SMOKE.

TRADITIONAL VOLCANO DANCERS OF VANUATU WITH MOUNT YASUR IN THE DISTANCE

STROMBOLI

STROMBOLI IS THE FIRST PLACE I EVER GOT TO SEE A VOLCANO ERUPTING. It was during my third year of college, when my volcanology class took a field trip to the island. We started climbing the mountain early in the afternoon. It was really hot, and it was very hard to get up to the top. I always say it was my head and not my legs that got me up there, because I wanted to see it so badly.

We reached the top of the crater at dusk. The first thing I remember about arriving was these deep, rumbling sounds. We were a loud group of about 20 students, and we'd been laughing and joking the whole time we were climbing the mountain. But when we heard those rumblings, we all got really quiet. We stood there and looked down inside the crater. Stromboli is known for giving regular bursts of lava every 10 or 15 minutes, from two different vents down at the bottom of the crater. One vent goes off, then the other one, and then it's quiet for a while. I looked down, and at first I could only see a dark, hilly, ash-covered landscape. It looked like a different world entirely. Then it started happening. A really tall lava fountain erupted from the first vent. There were lapilli (little stones of volcanic rock) falling back down into the crater, turning from red hot to dark black as they cooled off. Lava shot up at different heights, pulsating like a living creature. The volcano lit up the night sky, and I understood why Stromboli was called the Lighthouse of the Mediterranean. I couldn't look away. I didn't feel scared; my fascination overrode everything else.

We stayed and watched three eruptions before we made our way back down the volcano. My classmates had to drag me away because I didn't want to leave. When we left, we hiked down a different trail, covered with volcanic ash. It was like sliding down through sand. That whole experience was the highlight of my entire college education.

ARIANNA SOLDATI

NIGHTTIME FIREWORKS OF A STROMBOLI ERUPTION

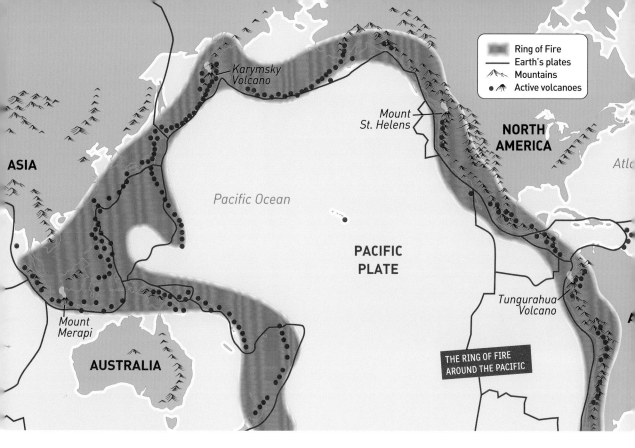

Ring of Fire
Earth's plates
Mountains
Active volcanoes

Karymsky
Volcano

Mount
St. Helens

NORTH
AMERICA

Atl

ASIA

Pacific Ocean

PACIFIC
PLATE

Tungurahua
Volcano

Mount
Merapi

AUSTRALIA

THE RING OF FIRE
AROUND THE PACIFIC

Longest String of Volcanoes

The 25,000-mile (40,234-km), horseshoe-shaped curve that roughly follows the Pacific coasts of Asia and North and South America is known as the Ring of Fire. Here lies the largest accumulation of volcanoes on Earth—a whopping 452 of them! In fact, 75 percent of all the active volcanoes that we know about are located here. This huge geographic area stretches from New Zealand, up into Japan, over and across Russia into Alaska, down the West Coast of the United States, then all the way to the southern tip of South America.

The Ring of Fire includes some of the most active and powerful volcanoes in the world, like Indonesia's Krakatau and, in the U.S., Alaska's Novarupta and Washington State's Mount St. Helens. What accounts for this incredible number of exploding mountains? The shifting tectonic plates on Earth's lithosphere. Three major

plates crash together here: the Eurasian plate, the Pacific plate, and the Indo-Australian plate. Other plates get jumbled up in the mix, too. This region is not only highly explosive but also very active, with 90 percent of our planet's earthquakes shaking things up in this region.

Just to the west of the westernmost edge of the Ring of Fire, in 2015 scientists discovered the longest chain of volcanoes found on a continent. Some 24 million years in the making, these are together known as the Cosgrove volcanic track. It stretches 1,200 miles (1,931 km) across Australia, over the Bass Strait, and onto the island of Tasmania. Why did it take researchers so long to discover these volcanoes and their relation to each other? They've been inactive for several million years and have worn away through time—so they were not as easy to notice.

The longest chain of related volcanoes that isn't found on a continent is the Hawaiian-Emperor

LAVA BOMB, MOUNT YASUR

WATCH OUT FOR LAVA BOMBS!

A LAVA BOMB IS A BLOB OF STILL SEMISOFT LAVA that gets ejected from a volcano after a blast and cools to rock before it hits the ground. It's just one of many dangers to people and animals living near active volcanoes. Lava bombs come in different sizes (although they're usually at least 2.5 inches [6.35 cm] in diameter). They also come in different textures and shapes. Bread-crust bombs have crackled surfaces. Ribbon bombs are long and stretched out. Spindle bombs have twisted ends. Spheroidal bombs are shaped like, well, spheres. Cow-pie bombs are flattened disks, like hockey pucks.

seamount chain. This group of mostly submarine volcanoes has formed as the Pacific plate shifts over a hot spot in the middle of the Pacific Ocean. Hot spots raise the temperature of the mantle, which forces lava up through fissures. The resulting chain that was formed in the Pacific Ocean is now the nine Hawaiian Islands, some of which are still very active today. Spanning a distance of 3,700 miles (5,955 km), this chain is more than three times as long as Cosgrove!

THE HAWAIIAN-EMPEROR SEAMOUNT CHAIN IS SHOWN HERE AS THE LIGHT BLUE DOTS IN THE DARK BLUE SEA.

The Strangest Volcanoes

These oddball creations will take your volcanic knowledge to the next level:

For starters, mud volcanoes. These often form when gases like methane start to accumulate underground, causing the mud lying above them to become pressurized and buoyant. This in turn makes cold mud either bubble to the surface of the Earth or explode. The mud dries into small cones that are usually only a few inches or a few feet high, although some grow to a few hundred feet. The most destructive and dramatic mud volcano of them all exploded on the island of Java in Indonesia in May 2006. It erupted over two square miles (5.2 square km), ling 20 people and causing $2.7 billion worth of damage. Some scientists think the explosion was triggered by engineers drilling for gas.

Mud volcanoes aren't the only odd ones out there. What do you get when you cross volcanoes with glaciers in icy volcanic places? Subglacial volcanoes! A subglacial volcano is one that erupts underneath a thick sheet of ice. Its hot lava melts some of the ice, which turns to water and quickly cools the lava into pillowy shapes. The melted glacier water can have a devastating effect, sometimes rising high enough to cause floods—called *jökulhlaups*. Iceland's Vatnajökull glacier has at least seven volcanoes lying beneath its surface. In British Columbia, in western Canada, scientists have figured out that the subglacial volcano Hoodoo Mountain erupts every 20,000 years or so. They believe the mountain is starting to get pretty close to its next eruption!

The term "lava lake" probably does not make you want to grab your bathing suit. These beds full of molten rock are giant vents that get fed a constant flow of lava from the magma chambers underneath them. Sometimes the lakes overflow, sending flamingly hot goo onto whatever happens to be at the foot of the volcano. Lava lakes are rare and extremely interesting to scientists.

LAVA LAKE IN HALEMAʻUMAʻU CRATER, KĪLAUEA

Researchers believe that if they can understand these lakes, they might be able to understand a lot more about how volcanoes work. In all, there are five lava lakes in the world. Kīlauea in Hawaii has two—one in a vent on its summit and the other in a vent on its side. A powerful and very active volcano called Erta Ale, in Ethiopia, has a lava lake, too. It has been filling up since 1906. Mount Nyiragongo, in the central African country of the Democratic Republic of the Congo, has a lava lake near its very high summit that's 1,970 feet (600 m) deep. And in Antarctica, the lava lake bubbling and puffing out smoke on Mount Erebus shoots out lava bombs at the researchers who come to study it.

QOBUSTAN MUD VOLCANO IN AZERBAIJAN, WHERE ONE-THIRD OF ALL MUD VOLCANOES CAN BE FOUND

VATNAJÖKULL GLACIER: THERE'S A VOLCANO UNDER THERE!

DEADLIEST ERUPTIONS

ONE WAY TO MEASURE THE POWER OF A VOLCANIC ERUPTION is to look at the impact on the people and communities nearby. We've marked the human toll of volcanic eruptions since people have been recording them. This history of deadly devastation is what has driven mankind to learn all they can about volcanoes. Here is a list of the top 10 deadliest eruptions we know about:

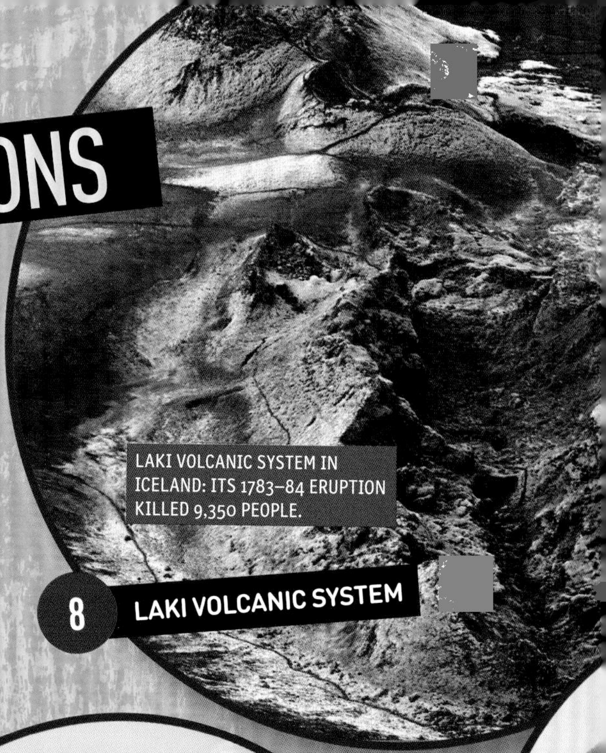

LAKI VOLCANIC SYSTEM IN ICELAND: ITS 1783–84 ERUPTION KILLED 9,350 PEOPLE.

8 LAKI VOLCANIC SYSTEM

10 MOUNT GALUNGGUNG

7 MOUNT VESUVIUS

MOUNT GALUNGGUNG IN INDONESIA: ITS 1882 ERUPTION KILLED 4,011 PEOPLE AND WIPED OUT 411 VILLAGES.

MOUNT VESUVIUS IN ITALY: ITS A.D. 79 ERUPTION KILLED 10,000 PEOPLE AND BURIED THE CITIES OF POMPEII AND HERCULANEUM.

9 MOUNT KELUD

MOUNT KELUD IN INDONESIA: ITS 1919 ERUPTION KILLED 5,110 PEOPLE AND WIPED OUT 100 VILLAGES.

6 SANTA MARÍA

SANTA MARÍA IN GUATEMALA: ITS 1902 ERUPTION KILLED 10,000 PEOPLE. THIS TIES IT WITH MOUNT KELUD'S 1586 ERUPTION.

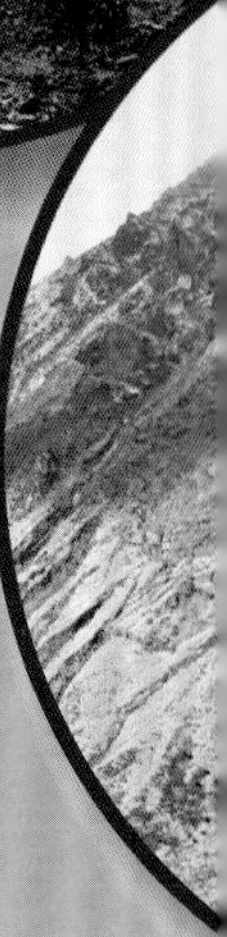

MOUNT KELUD IN INDONESIA (AGAIN): ITS 1586 ERUPTION ALSO KILLED 10,000 PEOPLE, AS DID SANTA MARÍA'S 1902 ERUPTION.

6 MOUNT KELUD

3 MOUNT PELÉE

MOUNT PELÉE IN MARTINIQUE: ITS 1902 ERUPTION KILLED 29,000 PEOPLE AND DESTROYED THE CITY OF SAINT-PIERRE.

5 MOUNT UNZEN

2 KRAKATAU

1 MOUNT TAMBORA

MOUNT TAMBORA IN INDONESIA: ITS 1815 ERUPTION KILLED AN ASTOUNDING 92,000 PEOPLE.

KRAKATAU IN INDONESIA: ITS 1883 ERUPTION KILLED 36,000 PEOPLE.

MOUNT UNZEN IN JAPAN: ITS 1792 ERUPTION KILLED BETWEEN 14,300 AND 15,000 PEOPLE.

4 NEVADO DEL RUIZ

NEVADO DEL RUIZ IN COLOMBIA: ITS 1985 ERUPTION, THE DEADLIEST IN MODERN TIMES, KILLED 23,000 PEOPLE AND BURIED A TOWN UNDER MUDFLOWS.

GET IN THE FLOW!

BUILD YOUR ROCK COLLECTION

Our world is made of rocks. A rock collection is an excellent way to build your geological expertise. Starting your collection can be as simple as looking down and recording what you see.

Here are some pro tips for creating a supercool rock collection:

1. **Create a field journal to log your observations.** You'll want to write down stuff like where you found your rock specimens and the descriptions of their size, color, shape, and texture. You'll also want to record similarities in the types of rocks you find in different locations.
2. **Devise a way to keep and label your specimens.** Some rock collectors use special boxes like the one you see here, but an old shoe box with cardboard dividers works just fine, too.
3. **Collect your specimens.** Interesting rocks are everywhere! Check out the rocks in your yard, at your school, or at the beach. Be sure to ask your parents if it's okay to keep what you find. There are a lot of places, like national parks or your neighbor's garden, where collecting rocks is not okay.
4. **Identify your rocks.** There are many books and resources in your local library that can help you figure out what kind of rocks you've found. A lot of libraries and museums have their own rock collections you can look at, too.

Are you ready to become a rock rock star?

GRANITE

RHYOLITE

RED GRANITE

GRANITE

FLINT

BASALT WITH QUARTZ VEINS

DIORITE

BASALT WITH QUARTZ VEINS

FIELD NOTES

Date: No:

<u>FOUND</u>

WHEN: THURSDAY AFTER SCHOOL

WHERE: AT THE PARK AROUND THE CORNER
UNDER THE SLIDE

<u>DESCRIPTION</u>

BASALT

SIZE: ABOUT 2" X 1"

SHAPE: KIND OF A MOON SHAPE

COLOR: GRAY, WITH FLECKS OF ORANGE & BLACK

OTHER NOTES: FEELS ROUGH AND BUMPY

ROCKS CAN BE FOUND
EVERYWHERE—EVEN AT
YOUR LOCAL PLAYGROUND!

KĪLAUEA'S PAHOEHOE
LAVA AT SUNSET

CHAPTER 2

VOLCANO BASICS

INTRODUCTION

I WENT TO PACAYA IN GUATEMALA DURING THE FIRST YEAR OF MY PH.D.

program. Pacaya is an active volcano, but it hadn't erupted in four years. That changed just before we got on the plane to Guatemala. The day before our flight, Pacaya started erupting!

ARIANNA SOLDATI

For the first two days after our arrival, we recorded videos of the lava flow to figure out how fast it was moving. Understanding how fast lava flows can help communities nearby know if people or property will be in its path. Turns out it was moving pretty fast, flowing between about 1 and 9 feet (0.3 to 2.8 m) per second—that's a pace of a slow walk up to a really fast run.

On the third day, we went around to the west side of the volcano, where there was fresh, hot lava—perfect for the samples we needed.

Later that day, we took a break for lunch and sat down on a big piece of volcanic rock. About midway through eating, we felt an earthquake. This one was not especially strong, and it lasted for only about ten seconds. But the feeling of an earthquake when you're on top of an active volcano is unsettling. And for it to happen while we were on this particular volcano was especially frightening.

Why? Because Pacaya has a crack that runs all the way across its top. The crack is aligned with a vent underneath. We think the mountain is actually splitting in half, and when that happens, it's going to be violent.

When I felt that earthquake, I thought, *Maybe the volcano is breaking apart right now. Should we leave?*

But no, we kept working. When you're doing fieldwork, you know you may not have a chance to come back to the same place again for years, so you want to accomplish all the work you planned to do. Plus, I was with my experienced advisor, who knew more than I did about the risk of the volcano breaking apart that day. I knew that if we'd felt more or stronger quakes, he would let us know it was time to get out of there. The whole experience was a good reminder that although volcanoes are fascinating, they can also be dangerous.

IRON-RICH PYROCLASTIC ROCK

LAVA ROCKS FROM PACAYA'S 2010 ERUPTION

WHEN I FELT THE EARTHQUAKE, I THOUGHT, MAYBE THE VOLCANO IS BREAKING APART RIGHT NOW.

AL VOLCAN
TO THE VOLCANO

ARIANNA TOOK THIS PICTURE OF PACAYA'S LAVA.

CLOSE YOUR EYES AND PICTURE A VOLCANO. WHAT DO YOU SEE?

You probably imagine a cone-shaped mountain erupting spectacularly with red-hot lava and fire, and billows of smoke and ash.

WHAT AN EARLY EARTH MAY HAVE LOOKED LIKE AS IT FORMED

This picture in your mind is accurate. But it's not the only picture of how a volcano looks and acts.

Volcanoes come in many shapes and sizes. Some don't even look like mountains at all. To look at the basics of what actually makes a volcano a *volcano,* we first have to travel back billions of years, to when Earth was forming.

The Making of a Volcano

Some 4.5 billion years ago, our now blue and water-topped planet was a hot, bubbling mess of magma, still working itself into a spherical shape. Melted metals and rocks, as well as gases, were all part of this crazy mix. Some of the metals in that bubbling stew—namely, iron and nickel—began to pull themselves together into a ball. This ball became Earth's core, or center, possibly about 1.5 billion years ago.

Swirling around that core was a sludge made of elements and compounds like garnet, magnesium oxide, iron, and potassium. This formed Earth's early mantle. Little by little, over millions of years, the thick, hot mantle layer cooled. The minerals inside it gave off water vapor, carbon dioxide, and nitrogen

in a process called outgassing. Outgassing helped harden the top of the mantle, which became an outer layer that cooled to form Earth's crust.

Outgassing also began to create our planet's atmosphere. And one theory is that this process made Earth warm enough to support the microscopic life that would eventually spring up. It even helped create our oceans. The water vapor that was released became liquid, which would become Earth's oceans.

What does any of this have to do with volcanoes? Everything! This is because volcanic activity is what caused the changes that made our planet billions of years ago.

Scientists still have lots of questions about the formation of the outermost parts of Earth. And lots of theories about it, too.

One theory is about the formation of tectonic plates. Tectonic plates are separate slabs of lithosphere that float on top of the upper mantle. (Tectonic comes from the Greek word *tekton,* which means "to build.") Scientists believe that older and cooler parts of the upper mantle were remelted by the heat deeper inside the planet. This made those bits of the

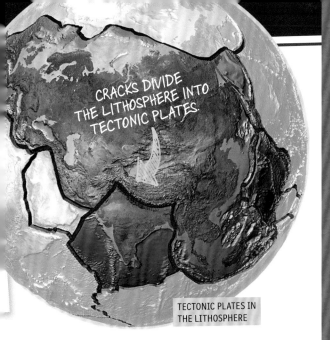

CRACKS DIVIDE THE LITHOSPHERE INTO TECTONIC PLATES.

TECTONIC PLATES IN THE LITHOSPHERE

crust and upper mantle—together called the lithosphere—weak, creating cracks in them. The cracks divided the lithosphere into its 15 major tectonic plates.

These plates actually shift around. They move only a few inches a year, but that's enough to make big things happen, such as the formation of volcanoes.

Sometimes the plates diverge, or pull away, from each other. This creates fissures, or cracks, that release lava through the crust. And then what do you get? Volcanoes, of course! In fact, fissures underwater can create mid-ocean ridges, forming wide underwater mountain chains!

Sometimes the plates converge, or crash, into each other, and one plate is caught beneath the other. This creates a subduction zone. In a subduction zone, the lower plate bends down toward the upper mantle and creates magma. The newly melted magma causes pressure that builds and pushes upward, breaking out onto the surface of Earth wherever it finds a weak spot in the crust. Ta-da, volcano!

This kind of convergence is happening with all those volcanoes in the Ring of Fire. In this case, the major Pacific plate and some smaller

EARTH'S LAYERS

OUR PLANET IS MADE UP OF THREE BASIC LAYERS: the core, mantle, and crust. But each of these layers has its own layers. Here's a close-up look from the inside out.

INNER CORE: Almost 4,000 miles (6,437 km) below Earth's surface. Scientists think the absolute center of the planet is probably a solid ball of iron and nickel, with a little silicon mixed in.

OUTER CORE: 3,000 miles (4,828 km) below Earth's surface. This is a layer of molten metal made up of iron and nickel.

CORE-MANTLE BOUNDARY: 1,802 miles (2,900 km) below Earth's surface. This is where the core ends and the mantle, which makes up 85 percent of Earth's weight and mass, begins.

LOWER MANTLE: Between 410 and 1,678 miles (660 and 2,700 km) below Earth's surface. It's incredibly hot down there, but even so, the rock that makes up the lower mantle is solid rather than liquid.

TRANSITION ZONE: Between 255 and 410 miles (410 and 660 km) below Earth's surface. You'll find very dense rocks here, as well as the minerals that hold the building blocks of water.

UPPER MANTLE: Between 62 and 255 miles (100 and 410 km) below Earth's surface. Here, the rocks are slightly melted—by temperatures that can reach 2570°F (1410°C).

CRUST: Made of moving tectonic plates that let magma bubble to the surface of the planet. The crust is three to five miles (4.8 to 8 km) thick under the oceans and up to 25 miles (40.2 km) thick under the continents. The crust is mainly made up of cooled magma.

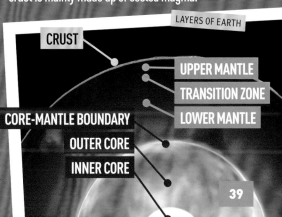

LAYERS OF EARTH

CRUST

UPPER MANTLE

TRANSITION ZONE

LOWER MANTLE

CORE-MANTLE BOUNDARY

OUTER CORE

INNER CORE

tectonic plates are getting pushed underneath or on top of each other.

In some places, the heat from the mantle rises up in an intense plume that melts the surrounding rock into magma, creating what's known as a hot spot. These hot spots can be found under the ocean and on land. They can create a thinning of Earth's crust, making it easier for the magma to melt through.

Hot spots happen at specific places where magma is formed. At the same time, the tectonic plates above the hot spots are always moving. This means that over time the hot spot creates a weak or thinning spot in the crust where the lava can flow out. The Hawaiian Islands were all formed—and are still being formed—by lava released from a hot spot in the middle of the Pacific Ocean. Eventually lava builds up into new land. This has been going on for 70 million years.

LAVA FLOWS OUT OF MOUNT KĪLAUEA IN HAWAII.

Types of Volcanoes

We know that volcanoes form differently thanks to all the ways that magma makes its way up to Earth's surface. But volcanoes also differ in how they look and erupt, and in what kinds of stuff shoots out of their vents. Some ooze. Some explode. Some erupt all the time, some hardly ever.

The type of volcano most people are familiar with is the cone-shaped mountain with steep sides that erupts by shooting lava from its top. A volcano like this is called a stratovolcano. It's also known as a composite volcano, because its outsides are *composed* of different layers of lava, ash, and rock—all the things that erupt out of it when it explodes.

Stratovolcanoes

Stratovolcanoes can grow to heights of around 8,000 feet (2,438 m). They are responsible for the

WHEN PLATE TECTONICS DON'T EQUAL VOLCANOES

IN ADDITION TO DIVERGING (pulling away) and converging (crashing), there's another way tectonic plates move: They rub up against each other. When the movement is particularly forceful, or sudden, earthquakes can happen. This movement doesn't create or release magma, so there's no volcanic eruption. But when an earthquake happens right underneath a volcano, it's probably caused by magma starting to move. These earthquakes are one way scientists know when a volcano is likely to blow.

SAN ANDREAS FAULT IN CALIFORNIA = EARTHQUAKES, NOT VOLCANOES

most violent eruptions on Earth. Mount St. Helens in Washington State is a stratovolcano. So are Mount Pinatubo, Mount Vesuvius, Krakatau, Mount Pelée, and Mount Etna—these are the world's deadliest exploders.

What makes stratovolcanoes so powerful? They erupt a kind of lava that has a lot of the mineral silica in it. The silica makes these lavas super sticky, which traps a lot of gas in them. When the trapped gas is looking for a way out, an eruption occurs.

Before that happens, though, the soon-to-be lava collects in a magma chamber. There, the pressure of the gas grows and grows. As the magma rises up inside the conduits and reaches the air, the pressure from the gas is finally released and—*kaboom!*

Only about half of what comes out during a stratovolcano eruption is actually lava. The rest of it is gas and a mixture of ash and rock fragments called tephra.

Stratovolcanoes, like any volcano, can have several vents, so when they explode, they can explode in multiple places and different directions. Look out ... *everywhere!*

WHAT'S UPWELLING?

MAGMA DOESN'T JUST EXIST AS A GIANT, FLAMING-HOT BLOB around Earth's middle. It's constantly being made and released by the movement of tectonic plates.

Tectonic plates converge and melt. The melted rock rises up from the mantle in an action called upwelling. Then it's released somewhere through Earth's crust. The plates then meet again, and the lower one sinks back down into the mantle and melts. It also melts the plate above, and the magma starts rising up all over again.

The circular, conveyor-belt-like motion of the rock sinking, melting, and then rising up again as magma makes the tectonic plates move. This process is what shifts continents, too.

Did you know that all the land on Earth used to be one giant continent called Pangaea? Over the course of about 70 million years, plate tectonics broke apart this one landmass into two landmasses. Those two broke apart again and again over the next 150 million years, resulting in the seven continents we have today.

SANTIAGUITO DOME AT STRATOVOLCANO SANTA MARÍA, GUATEMALA

UPWELLING IS A PROCESS THAT DRIVES THE FLOW OF THE MAGMA AND THE MOVEMENT OF EARTH'S PLATES.

CROSS SECTION OF A VOLCANO

ALL VOLCANOES HAVE FOUR THINGS in common: a **SOURCE AREA** where rock melts into magma, a **MAGMA CHAMBER** where magma gathers, a kind of a pipe called a **CONDUIT** that the magma rises through, and a **CRATER** with at least one vent in it, out of which the conduit releases the magma (now called lava). Here's what it looks like:

MAGMA TURNING TO LAVA AS IT FLOWS OR ERUPTS OUT OF THE CRATER AT THE TOP OF THE VOLCANO, ALONG WITH ASH, GAS, AND ROCKS

MAGMA RISING VIA CONDUIT FROM THE MAGMA CHAMBER THROUGH THE ROCK-SIDED VOLCANO

CRUST WITH MAGMA CHAMBER, WHERE MAGMA ACCUMULATES

MANTLE WHERE MAGMA IS FORMED

Stratovolcano Profile:
Mount Pinatubo, Luzon, Philippines

It was fast asleep for 600 years. Then, in 1991, Mount Pinatubo woke up. Some scientists think that a massive earthquake 60 miles (100 km) away shook the mighty mountain awake when it rumbled in July 1990. That distant quake caused some small earthquakes at Pinatubo. Then it seemed to go back to sleep. But several months later, another series of earthquakes forced steam to blast out of Pinatubo's vents, creating three new craters in its sides. For weeks, thousands of earthquakes rumbled under the mountain's belly, and it burped out noxious sulfur dioxide gas. Then magma began oozing out to form a lava dome. It was all going pretty slowly—until finally, on June 12, 1991, the whole thing exploded.

A jet of gassy lava shot out of the volcano's crater. An enormous ash cloud, 20 miles (32.2 km) high, rose into the sky. As if that wasn't bad enough, a typhoon—a powerful tropical storm—hit the island of Luzon on the very same day. Powerful winds from the typhoon blew ash in every direction, for miles and miles. The sky turned black in the middle of the afternoon. Avalanches of gas, ash, mud, and rocks sped down the mountain's side, burying the world around it in thick sludge.

The eruption of Mount Pinatubo was the second most powerful of the 20th century. It released such huge amounts of gas and ash that it blocked out the rays of the sun and cooled our entire planet by almost one degree for several months. Still, thanks to all of Pinatubo's early warning signs, scientists were able to predict the eruption before it happened. Many people were evacuated, and many lives were saved.

PHOTO OF MOUNT PINATUBO ERUPTING IN 1991

CINDER CONES INSIDE HALEAKALĀ CRATER, MAUI, HAWAII

Cinder Cone Volcanoes

Cinder cone volcanoes are smaller and weaker than stratovolcanoes. They are also simpler in the way they work. That's because cinder cone volcanoes contain only one vent for the lava to erupt out of. They have steep, sloping sides, and they don't usually grow much taller than a few hundred feet (100 m). When they blow lava through their vents, the lava comes out in small pieces, or cinders, as it whooshes through the air. The cooled-off cinders fall back down around the vent, creating a cone around it—a cinder cone. (This is how cinder cone volcanoes got their name!)

TEARDROP-SHAPED LAVA CALLED PELE'S TEARS

Parícutin in Mexico may be the world's most famous cinder cone volcano. That's because it grew right before people's eyes. In the afternoon of February 20, 1943, it popped out of the middle of a cornfield, rising six feet (2 m) as farmers watched. That same day it exploded with ash and gas until about

TYPES OF TEPHRA

TEPHRA, A MIX OF ASH AND ROCK FRAGMENTS, comes in all different shapes and sizes—from huge blocks to powdery ash. The larger the pieces of tephra shooting out during an eruption, the closer they fall to the volcano. The smallest pieces travel many miles and make it hard for people and animals to breathe. Here's a rundown of the different types of tephra:

BLOCKS AND BOMBS: The largest pieces of tephra can be angular (blocks) or rounded (bombs) chunks of lava that harden into rocks as they fly through the air. When a lot of gas escapes from the lava, it creates lightweight, porous bombs of rock called pumice—the only rock that can float.

VOLCANIC BOMB FROM MONTAÑA COLORADA, CANARY ISLANDS

LAPILLI: These small rocks are about the size of walnuts. The word "lapilli" means "little stones" in Latin.

PELE'S TEARS and **PELE'S HAIR:** Named for the Hawaiian goddess of volcanoes, these flecks of lava can cool into teardrop shapes called Pele's tears. If they are pulled by the wind into thin strands as they fly, they become Pele's hair.

ASH: This is the smallest type of tephra. Powdery bits of glass, crystal, and rock make up ash that can travel far and wide, sometimes burying cars, houses, plants, and even whole hillsides. If ash makes it all the way up into Earth's atmosphere, it becomes electrically charged and can cause lightning.

midnight. After the initial explosion, the real eruption began and lasted for the next nine years, with the mountain around it growing to a total of 1,391 feet (424 m) high. Then, in 1952, Parícutin stopped erupting. It's now considered extinct because there's no longer a source of magma to erupt. It was the first, and one of the only, volcanoes scientists have been able to study from birth to extinction.

Cinder Cone Profile: Cerro Negro, Nicaragua

Cerro Negro is a picture-perfect cinder cone volcano. It's shaped like an upside-down bowl, topped with a big crater. All the built-up sandy cinders that give it its shape also give it a soft black color. Cerro Negro is actually one of four cinder cones that exist in the same mountainous region of Nicaragua, not far from another volcano, called Las Pilas.

Cerro Negro is now over 800 feet (244 m) tall. But it's been growing and shaping itself since it

first exploded in 1850. It has erupted 20 times since then, once every few years. This makes it the most active—as well as the youngest—volcano in Central America.

The last time Cerro Negro erupted was August 7, 1999. That eruption started off with hundreds of small earthquakes shaking in the middle of the night. The next morning, Cerro Negro started exploding, with 23,000-foot (7,010-m) ash clouds and 1,000-foot (305-m) lava fountains. The explosions happened every few seconds for two days, popping out of four new vents that opened up in its crater. The volcano put on quite a show!

CINDER CONE VOLCANO, PARÍCUTIN, MEXICO

Shield Volcanoes

Some of the biggest volcanoes are shield volcanoes. Unlike stratovolcanoes that are really tall, shield volcanoes are often super wide, with gently sloping sides. Some shield volcanoes are miles wide at their bases. That's because shield

CLOUDS OF ASH ERUPTING FROM CERRO NEGRO IN NICARAGUA

ENORMOUS SHIELD VOLCANO MAUNA KEA IN HAWAII

volcanoes don't explode violently like stratovolcanoes and cinder cone volcanoes. Their lava flows out gently and easily, and can travel long distances before it starts to cool and harden. Sometimes their lava also seeps out from vents in the sides of their cones. This allows the lava to travel even farther.

Shield volcano lavas are usually made out of basalt. This black-colored rock contains two kinds of minerals, called feldspar and pyroxene, which both contain silica. Basalt is very hard, and it's the most common kind of rock on our planet—and on our moon, too.

SMOKE RISING FROM ERTA ALE IN ETHIOPIA

Shield Volcano Profile: Erta Ale, Ethiopia

At 2,000 feet (610 m) tall and 31 miles (50 km) wide, Erta Ale isn't the tallest or the widest shield volcano on Earth, but it is one of the most interesting. It's been continuously erupting since 1967, and it has one of only five lava lakes in the world. The lake sits inside the summit's crater, which is 300 feet (91.4 m) deep, and is fed 1800°F (982°C) magma around the clock.

In January 2017, the lava lake became full. At first, lava fountains spurted from the crater just a few feet into the air. But these fountains quickly grew to almost 200 feet (61 m) high. Visitors reported seeing waves of lava crashing against the edge of the crater. The waves spilled over Erta Ale's top, forming rivers of lava that rolled down its sides at 45 miles (72.4 km) an hour. As lava drained out of the lake, Erta Ale's crater partially collapsed in several places, making the volcano look totally different than it had at the beginning of the lava overflow.

Scientists are keeping a close watch on Erta Ale to see what it will do next.

Calderas

A caldera (Spanish for "cauldron") is what you get when the outside structure of a volcano

A LAVA FOUNTAIN SPURTS FROM ERTA ALE'S LAVA LAKE IN ETHIOPIA.

BUBBLING MUD POTS,
UZON CALDERA IN SIBERIA

collapses. This happens when the magma chamber under the mountain partially empties out—usually violently and explosively, but sometimes over the course of several eruptions. Afterward, the earth under the mountain's base is partially hollow and can't support its weight. So the mountain slumps and falls inward. What's left behind is a giant bowl in the ground.

Yellowstone National Park sits inside a humongous caldera. And a mega magma chamber sits right underneath. It is probably filling up with hot magma as you read this. Will it erupt again? Probably. But we don't know when. If and when it does, scientists will refer to it as a supervolcano, because the force of its eruption will be so powerful, it could affect the climate around the world for many years.

SEMERU VOLCANO ERUPTING BEHIND THE TENGGER CALDERA IN JAVA

Caldera Profile: Uzon Caldera, Siberia, Russia

About 40,000 years ago, a volcano in the vast wilderness of Siberia, in eastern Russia, collapsed after numerous eruptions. What was left behind was a caldera 10 miles (16 km) in diameter. Over time, part of it filled with water, creating lakes. Some of these lakes never ice over, even though Siberia is totally freezing in the winter. Their waters are kept warm by the magma-heated gases that still rise up where the volcano used to stand.

This same heat causes geysers to shoot hot-water fountains in the air. It also creates boiling mud pots. One of these steaming mud cauldrons bubbles up every few seconds, twisting its glop into sculpted rose shapes. They may be beautiful, but the hot bubbling and splattering mud can also be dangerous to anyone—or anything—nearby.

WHY VOLCANOES ACT THE WAY THEY DO

THERE'S ONE MAIN THING that determines whether a volcano oozes or explodes: gas bubbles. All magma contains gas of one kind or another, like carbon dioxide or water vapor. As magma rises through a conduit, the gas depressurizes, like bubbles in a bottle of soda when you shake it. Then the gas tries to escape from the magma. If the gas has no trouble doing this, the gas forms bubbles, which pop. Then the magma oozes up and out of the volcano. If the gas has a hard time escaping, its bubbles stay stuck in the magma. When the magma travels up through the conduit of the volcano and hits the air, the bubbles explode. The more bubbles that are trapped in the magma as it shoots out, the more explosive an eruption will be.

VIOLENT EXPLOSION OF LAVA, ASH, AND STEAM, KALAPANA, KĪLAUEA, HAWAII

It's Alive! Or Is It?

The types of volcanoes we've been talking about can be active or extinct. What's the difference? An active volcano can still erupt and has erupted at least once in the last 10,000 years. They still have magma pooling under their base, which could lead to an eruption.

An extinct volcano has no magma left in its chamber and the conditions where new magma could form no longer exist.

But here's the catch: Extinct volcanoes have come back to life when no one thought they would or could. One example of this is Sotará in Colombia. In June 2012, after being considered extinct for no one knows how long, it started rumbling with as many as 150 earthquakes a day. Prediction: This volcano is going to blow ... one day.

EXTINCT VOLCANO MOUNT BISOKE (RWANDA & DEMOCRATIC REPUBLIC OF THE CONGO)

Types of Eruptions

We know there are different kinds of volcanoes. There are also different ways those volcanoes erupt: fast, slow, powerful, or oozy. Mostly, the kinds of eruptions get their names from the places where scientists first studied them. They fit into two basic categories: effusive, where lava flows out gently and easily, and explosive.

Hawaiian Eruption

First up in our eruption roundup: the Hawaiian eruption. This is the gentlest of all possible volcanic eruptions. It's named for the kind of volcanic activity that's found on the Hawaiian Islands. When volcanoes like Kīlauea and Mauna Loa erupt, they may spurt spectacular fire fountains up into the air, some of which can last for days. But that's about as violent as they get.

THE VOGS OF KĪLAUEA

YOU'VE HEARD OF FOG. You've heard of smog. What the heck is *vog*? It's volcanic smog. When Kīlauea erupts, it lets out gases like sulfur dioxide, as well as water vapor and carbon dioxide. All this mixes in the atmosphere with volcanic dust, oxygen, and sunlight. Then it turns into fine particles that make the air hazy and hard to breathe. Hawaii has *vog* alerts—like summertime heat alerts or air pollution alerts—to let residents know when the air quality will be bad because of vog.

KĪLAUEA IN HAWAII: A CLASSIC HAWAIIAN ERUPTION

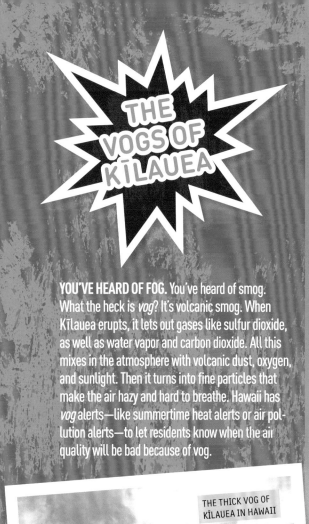

THE THICK VOG OF KĪLAUEA IN HAWAII

LAVA FLOWING INTO THE OCEAN NEAR KALAPANA IN HAWAII

However, lava flows out of their craters and spills over the land, sometimes traveling great distances. The longest distance ever recorded for lava from one of these volcanoes was 35 miles (56.3 km). That flow came out of Mauna Loa in 1859.

Pele's tears and Pele's hair are commonly found with Hawaiian-style eruptions.

Strombolian Eruptions

Strombolian eruptions feature much taller lava fountains, which can reach a few hundred feet (about 100 meters or more) in the air. And these fountains might have some ash and bomb- or lapilli-size rocks mixed in. Lavas from Strombolian eruptions don't really flow. They burst out of craters in loud, bright blasts. They may be noisy and create an exciting light show, but like Hawaiian eruptions, they're not very dangerous because the eruptions tend to be small. They get their name from the volcano named Stromboli on the Italian island of Stromboli, in the Tyrrhenian Sea just north of Sicily. Stromboli has been erupting every 15 minutes or so, nonstop, for hundreds of years.

A STROMBOLIAN ERUPTION AT TUNGURAHUA IN ECUADOR

ANAK KRAKATAU IN INDONESIA GIVES OFF VULCANIAN ERUPTIONS.

Vulcanian Eruptions

When a volcano stops erupting, lava can cool and harden inside its conduit, forming a plug. Or it can build up over a vent, in a formation called a lava dome. Then the next time the volcano is set to erupt, its sticky, gas-filled magma has to push past this plug or lava dome. What you then get is a short but really explosive eruption called a Vulcanian eruption.

Vulcanian eruptions are super powerful, sending lava and tephra a mile (1.6 km) or more up into the air at speeds of 800 miles (1,287 km) per hour. They don't happen often, but when they do, they are extremely violent and can last a few days. This type of eruption is named for another volcanic island in Italy: Vulcano.

PLINIAN ERUPTION AT MOUNT ST. HELENS

They have supergassy, supersticky magma that explodes when it reaches the air. And they release thick, mushroom-shaped columns of ash and lapilli 35 miles (56.3 km) into the atmosphere. Winds can carry this mixture for miles, covering roads, houses, and towns, and showering lava bombs for several miles over the landscape. Though they are really destructive, this type of eruption empties the magma chamber in one go. That means they're not likely to erupt again right away.

Plinian eruptions are named for a Roman historian known as Pliny the Younger. In A.D. 79, he described watching the eruption of Mount Vesuvius, which destroyed the ancient city of Pompeii.

Plinian Eruptions

Plinian eruptions are the hotshots of volcanic explosions. They are powerful, loud, and deadly.

Phreatomagmatic Eruptions

There is one more category of eruptions. This one takes place when magma mixes with water. Called phreatomagmatic eruptions, this type of

BLAM! UNDERSEA SURTSEYAN ERUPTION OFF THE COAST OF TONGA

PYROCLASTIC FLOWS FROM MOUNT ETNA, SICILY, ITALY

eruption happens when magma has to cross water to get to Earth's surface. These eruptions occur with underwater volcanoes and with volcanoes on land that are covered in glaciers. Depending on the amount of magma and water, we classify phreatomagmatic eruptions as phreatic (having a lot of water and little magma) or Surtseyan (having little water and a lot of magma).

When the spurting lava makes it through the water and hits the air, the water around the lava turns to steam and explodes. *Blam!* During Surtseyan eruptions, plumes of ash and gas pour out, and bunches of tephra get flung around. If these volcanoes keep erupting, their craters get higher and higher, moving farther above the surface of the water.

LAHARS (HERE, AT NEVADO DEL RUIZ) ARE SERIOUSLY DESTRUCTIVE.

When this happens, they can change into volcanoes with Hawaiian-style eruptions. Surtseyan eruptions are named for the island of Surtsey, off the coast of Iceland.

Volcano Features

As much as the varied forms and types of eruptions make volcanoes fascinating, the different features of volcanoes can make each one truly unique.

One of these features is a lava lake. A lava lake occurs when lava flows out and pools in a volcano's vents or craters. Some lakes, like the one at Erta Ale in Ethiopia, can bubble up with hot lava for months or even years. From time to time, a lava lake can form a thin crust on

A'A VS. PAHOEHOE LAVA

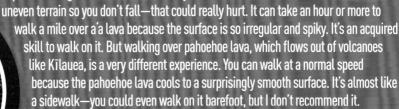

THE FIRST DAY I WAS AT PACAYA VOLCANO in Guatemala, my fieldwork group went on a hike to an active lava flow. To get there, we had to walk across older, solidified lava flows. Pacaya erupts a'a lava, which has a ton of gas bubbles in it. When you walk on recently released a'a lava, you can feel how this *gassy* lava becomes *glassy* when it cools. It makes a *clink, clink* sound under your feet, and it's as sharp as broken glass. You have to be really careful on the uneven terrain so you don't fall—that could really hurt. It can take an hour or more to walk a mile over a'a lava because the surface is so irregular and spiky. It's an acquired skill to walk on it. But walking over pahoehoe lava, which flows out of volcanoes like Kīlauea, is a very different experience. You can walk at a normal speed because the pahoehoe lava cools to a surprisingly smooth surface. It's almost like a sidewalk—you could even walk on it barefoot, but I don't recommend it. One thing geologists experience as they trek across any kind of cooled lava is that their backpacks get heavier as they walk. Why? Because geologists are constantly collecting rocks as they go!

ARIANNA SOLDATI

GASSY A'A LAVA TURNS GLASSY WHEN IT COOLS.

its top that eventually breaks off and sinks back into the lava.

Not all volcanic flows are the same, either. Pyroclastic flows are fast-moving rivers of volcanic gas, rock, ash, and debris. They run over everything in their path, burying obstacles or carrying them along as they move at top speeds of 50 miles (80.5 km) an hour. It's common for pyroclastic flows to set on fire the objects they pass—because pyroclastic flows can reach temperatures of 1300°F (704°C).

Just as destructive as pyroclastic flows, lahars bulldoze their way across land. *Lahar* is an Indonesian word that refers to a mixture of water and volcanic ash. Basically, lahars are giant mudslides. They can be observed rolling swiftly down

PAHOEHOE LAVA IS SMOOTH AND ROPY.

the sides of stratovolcanoes, picking up rocks, dirt, and even trees as they go. As lahars begin to slow down, they leave behind all the debris they've picked up, making a huge mess. They can also leave deep piles of mud in rivers or streams, which can lead to flooding.

All About Lava

Sure, most volcanic eruptions are unique. As we've already seen, they can spurt gas or steam or ash, and rocks of all sizes. But most have one thing in common: lava.

Many of the lavas on Earth are made out of fine-grained rock called basalt. There are three main kinds of basaltic lava flows. One type of lava flow is pahoehoe (that's pronounced paw-HOO-ee-hoo-ee). *Hoe* is a

UNDERWATER PILLOW LAVA IS PUFFY AND BULBOUS.

BLOCK LAVA IS MADE OF ANDESITE LAVA THAT FORMS ANGULAR CHUNKS WITH SMOOTH SIDES WHEN IT COOLS.

RHYOLITE LAVA IS SUPERSTICKY.

Hawaiian word that means "to paddle." When you paddle a canoe, for example, your oar makes a swirly shape in the water as you push it. And a swirly shape is a characteristic of pahoehoe lava. It's also described as being smooth and ropy, like brownie batter being poured into a pan.

Pahoehoe is the kind of lava flow you usually find coming out of Hawaiian and other shield volcanoes. It flows slowly and easily over flat surfaces and gentle slopes because it doesn't have a lot of gas trapped inside it. Since it moves so slowly, it has time to cool a little and build up a protective skin over its hot insides. This skin traps in the heat and allows the lava to keep moving underneath.

The second type of flow is the aʻa lava flow. Aʻa (pronounced AH-ah) is also a Hawaiian word, meaning "to burn." Aʻa lava flows out of volcanoes during eruptions, but then it moves slowly down steep slopes because it has a lot of gas trapped inside it. It also cools quickly, which makes aʻa lava thick and sticky. This quick cooling also creates a crust that tears as the lava moves. The pieces of crust get sucked back into the flow and make aʻa lava chunky. It cools in blocks or spiny shapes.

A volcano can eject pahoehoe lava during one eruption and aʻa lava during another—or even change from pahoehoe to aʻa during the same eruption. If the force of the eruption and the steepness of the slope change, then the lava flow does, too. However, once pahoehoe turns to aʻa, it isn't able to clump back into pahoehoe.

The third type of lava flow is called pillow lava flow. Pillow lava comes out of some underwater volcanic flows. It's puffy and bulbous and has a thick crust because the water cools it down extrafast. The lava billows out of vents, then cools on the vents' outsides into lobe-like shapes. As more lava gets pushed out from behind, the crust cracks and more lobes billow

CARBONATITE LAVA ERUPTS BLACK, TURNS CHALK WHITE, THEN, WITHIN A FEW MONTHS, DISINTEGRATES INTO POWDER.

RARE CARBONATITE LAVA FLOWING FROM OL DOINYO LENGAI IN TANZANIA

out of the first lobe. When an eruption is over, it can leave behind formations of lava that are hundreds of feet thick.

Most often lava is made of basalt, though block lava is different. It is made of a rock called andesite, which is extremely thick and sticky when it's melted. Block lava is usually ejected from stratovolcanoes but doesn't flow very far. When it cools, it has smooth sides and an angular, blocky shape.

Stratovolcanoes can eject rhyolite lava, too. Rhyolite is a light-colored rock that's made up mostly of silica and contains potassium and sodium. This makes rhyolite lava supersticky. When it is ejected, it mostly oozes out of vents and forms lava domes when it cools.

Komatiite lavas have very little silica but a lot of magnesium oxide. They are thin, almost watery, as they flow. These lavas don't seem to

ALMOST WATERY AS IT FLOWS: KOMATIITE LAVA

be erupting anymore, though. The "youngest" example of komatiite lava that scientists have found is 90 million years old, from an extinct volcano in what's now Colombia. It cooled into lacy patterns made up of crystals.

The rarest lava is carbonatite lava. It has a lot of calcium, sodium, and carbon dioxide in it and can erupt at superlow temperatures (around 1000°F [538°C], as opposed to 2100°F [1149°C] for regular old basaltic lava). This makes it really loose and runny, so it erupts in a way that some people have described as like water coming out of a hose. Carbonatite lava erupts black, and then, as it dries, it turns chalk white, giving a ghostly appearance to the landscape. Within a few months, it disintegrates into powder. There's only one volcano on our planet that erupts carbonatite lava: Ol Doinyo Lengai in Tanzania.

EXPLOSIVE VOLCANOES

ACCORDING TO THE GLOBAL VOLCANISM PROGRAM in Washington, D.C., there have been eight confirmed eruptions that came close to maxing out the Volcanic Explosivity Index (VEI), a scale from 0 to 8 that scientists use to measure the power of an eruption. Here we've mapped all eight of these VEI-7 eruptions. Our explorer Arianna has been to one, Crater Lake in the U.S., and she hopes to visit more of them. Check out all the other volcanoes she's been to—that's a lot of lava!

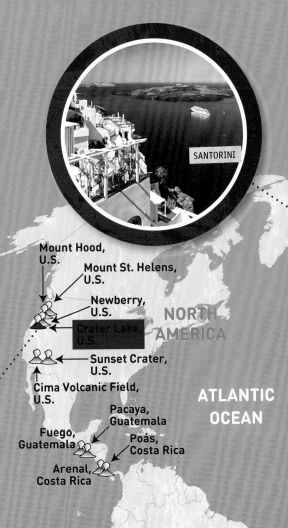

SANTORINI

Mount Hood, U.S.

Mount St. Helens, U.S.

Newberry, U.S.

Crater Lake, U.S.

Sunset Crater, U.S.

Cima Volcanic Field, U.S.

Kīlauea, U.S.

Pacaya, Guatemala

Fuego, Guatemala

Poás, Costa Rica

Arenal, Costa Rica

NORTH AMERICA

ATLANTIC OCEAN

CRATER LAKE

PACIFIC OCEAN

SOUTH AMERICA

Cerro Blanco, Argentina

CERRO BLANCO

MAP KEY

- Visited by Arianna
- VEI-7 eruption

CHANGBAISHAN

KURILE LAKE

ARCTIC OCEAN

EUROPE

ASIA

Chaîne
des Puys,
France

Vesuvius,
Italy

Stromboli,
Italy

Vulcano,
Italy

Mount Etna,
Italy

Santorini,
Greece

Kurile Lake,
Russia

Changbaishan,
China-North Korea

Kikai Caldera,
Japan

PACIFIC
OCEAN

INDIAN
OCEAN

Rinjani Samalas,
Indonesia

Tambora,
Indonesia

Piton de La Fournaise,
La Réunion (France)

KIKAI CALDERA

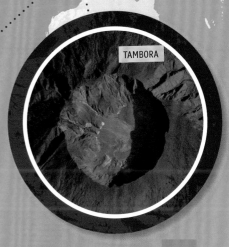
TAMBORA

RINJANI SAMALAS

GET IN THE FLOW!

MIX AND MATCH LAVA

DIFFERENT VOLCANOES erupt with different kinds of lava. Match the type of lava to its description.

A. PUFFY AND BULBOUS, FROM COOLING UNDERWATER

B. DRIES INTO PALE DOMES

C. SMOOTH AND ROPY

D. ERUPTS BLACK, DRIES WHITE, AND TURNS TO POWDER

E. DRIES INTO LACY CRYSTALS

F. CHUNKY AND SPINY

G. SMOOTH-SIDED AND BLOCKY

1 PAHOEHOE

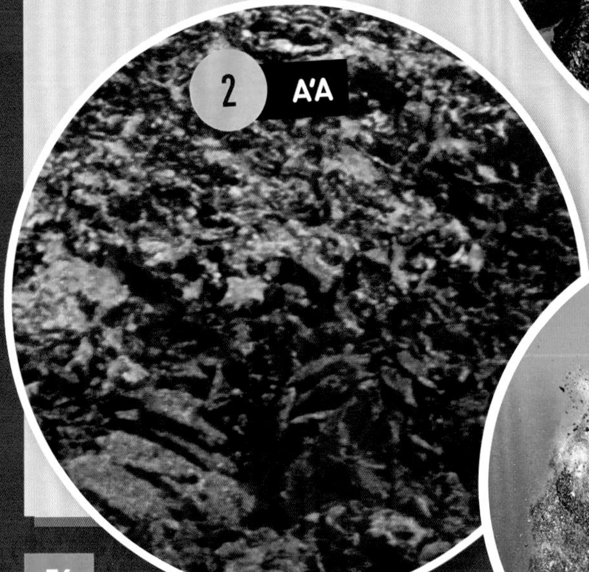

2 A'A

3 PILLOW

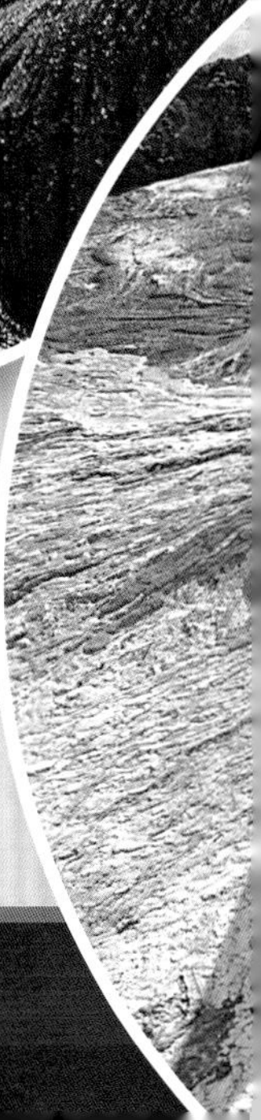

4 BLOCK

5 RHYOLITE

7 CARBONATITE

6 KOMATIITE

VOLCANOES, LIKE BATUR IN BALI, HELP MAKE THE LAND FERTILE.

CHAPTER 3
LIVING WITH VOLCANOES

INTRODUCTION

A LOT OF PEOPLE LIVE NEAR AND AROUND VOLCANOES,

and some of these areas are so beautiful that people travel from all over to enjoy them. The Chaîne des Puys (SHEN de pwee) in central France is a perfect example.

ARIANNA SOLDATI

It's a chain of about 70 volcanoes in the middle of the Auvergne region. But these volcanoes may not be what you expect. They look more like a series of green hills than a chain of volcanoes. Craters are the only feature you can see that gives you a clue these are volcanoes.

There are many different types of volcanoes in the chain. Some of them are cinder cones, and some are maars—that is, a kind of shallow crater that's formed when magma and water meet to make a steam explosion. Others have lakes in their craters, and some of them are volcanic domes. The cool thing about these volcanoes is that they are mono-genetic. That means they erupt once. Then, after that first eruption, they never erupt again in the same spot. The next time an eruption goes off in the chain, it happens in a slightly different place.

The Chaîne des Puys—which means "chain of volcanic hills"—volcanoes are all pretty short compared to other volcanoes. The tallest is Puy de Dôme, at 4,803 feet (1,464 m) tall. The last eruption in the chain was about 70,000 years ago, which isn't a long time in terms of geology. Eruptions could happen again anytime.

These days Chaîne des Puys is one of the most popular vacation areas in France. People come from all over to enjoy the hikes and hot springs in the area. Hiking Puy de Dôme is easy, even for kids. In about an hour, you're at the top. From there you can see volcanoes all around you. It's really beautiful. If you can't hike it, you can take a train to the top instead.

The volcanic ash makes the soil in the region very fertile for growing crops like grapes, lentils, barley wheat, and sweet corn. People in the area use volcanic rocks, mainly made of black basalt, for construction. There's a church built out of it, and many other buildings are completely black because they're made out of the rocks, too. The region also has very clean water because the water is filtered and purified as it flows through the basalt.

SCORIA FLOW

PYROCLASTIC FLOW

LAYERS OF SOIL SHOWING THE HISTORY OF VOLCANIC EVENTS AT CHAÎNE DES PUYS IN FRANCE

THE CHAÎNE DES PUYS VOLCANOES ARE **MONOGENETIC.** THAT MEANS THEY **ERUPT ONCE,** THEN NEVER AGAIN IN THE SAME SPOT.

AL VOLCAN
TO THE VOLCANO

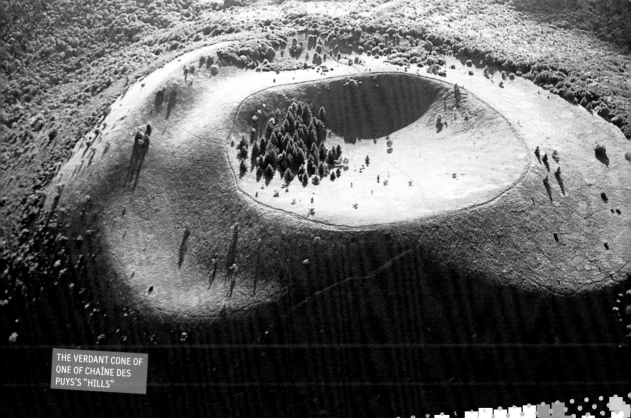

THE VERDANT CONE OF ONE OF CHAÎNE DES PUYS'S "HILLS"

HUMANS HAVE LIVED WITH AND TOLD STORIES ABOUT VOLCANOES

for millions of years. We've watched them erupt with both fear and wonder.

We've lived with the results of their fury: rivers of lava and clouds of ash, earthquakes and tsunamis, temperature drops and darkened skies. We've also benefited from the rich nutrients they bring to our soils and from their creation of new land formations—including the Hawaiian Islands!

All around the world, from Alaska to Greece to Japan—and everywhere in between—people once used storytelling to explain these unpredictable, exploding mountains. These stories from our past aren't just fantastic legends. Modern-day archaeologists and volcanologists think some of these stories contain important clues to eruptions from long ago, which can help us understand the eruptions we experience today, and how people today live in the shadow of these nearby volcanoes.

Humans, Volcanoes, and Myths

A long time ago, before we had scientific explanations for figuring out the world around us, we had stories. Our ancestors told stories that explained the things they saw around them: the stars in the sky, night and day, seasons, the colors of birds, and yes—volcanoes and their eruptions.

There are a lot of places in North America that have active volcanoes. The people in those areas have thought about and explained the volcanoes around them in many ways. The Klickitat (pronounced klik-i-tat) tribe in what is now Washington State tell a story about a beautiful maiden named Loowit. She was loved by two brothers, Wy'east and Klickitat. The brothers fought for Loowit. The brothers' father, Sahale, the Great Spirit, grew tired of their fighting and punished his sons by turning one into what is now called Mount Hood and one into what is

ALPENGLOW CREATES GOLD AND PINK LIGHT ON THE PEAKS AND VALLEYS OF MOUNT SHASTA IN CALIFORNIA.

now Mount Adams. The maiden he turned into what is now Mount St. Helens.

In what is now Northern California, the Modoc Indians believed that the stratovolcano Mount Shasta was created when the Chief of the Sky Spirits drilled a hole in the sky. Snow and ice fell through the hole and onto the ground. This piled up into Mount Shasta, where the Chief built a house and moved in with his family. When the Chief tossed logs onto his fire, the ground rumbled and the mountain threw off sparks and ash.

In another myth, told by the Klamath Indians, Skell, the Chief of the Above World, stood on top of Mount Shasta. One hundred miles (161 km) away, in what is now Oregon, Llao, the Chief of the Below World, stood on top of another stratovolcano, Mount Mazama. The two chiefs threw rocks and fire at each other until Llao fell back into the Below World. This made a huge hole in the ground that

TI LEAF OFFERING TO PELE AT HALEMA'UMA'U, HAWAII

eventually filled with water. This is how legend says Mount Mazama's Crater Lake was made.

More than 5,000 miles (8,047 km) from Mount Mazama, and across the Pacific Ocean, native Hawaiians have celebrated their goddess of fire, Pele, for many generations. Pele features prominently in the legends about the volcanic eruptions that abound in the Hawaiian Islands. In one of them, Pele lived in a steaming crater called Halema'uma'u, on the island of Kīlauea. She sent one of her sisters to go out and find the man she was in love with. When her sister took too long to retrieve him, Pele believed her sister had stolen him. Then Pele set her sister's forests on fire in revenge.

Some Hawaiians say the only way to get on Pele's good side is to visit her in her crater with offerings of food and flowers!

According to Aztec legend, the Mexican volcanoes Iztaccihuatl and Popocatépetl (pronounced its-TAK-see-wattle and po-po-ka-te-PET-l) were

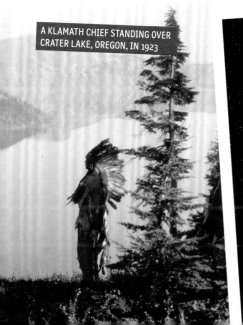

A KLAMATH CHIEF STANDING OVER CRATER LAKE, OREGON, IN 1923

HAWAII'S HALEMA'UMA'U CRATER AT NIGHT

A WOMAN WHO WAS REALLY A GODDESS RETURNED TO MOUNT FUJI.

once star-crossed lovers. When Popocatépetl was away at battle, Iztaccihuatl was tricked by a rival of Popocatépetl into believing that he had been killed. She died in despair. Popocatépetl returned home and found Iztaccihuatl dead. Anguished, he built a mountain as a tomb for her and set it on fire. Then he changed himself into a mountain to watch over Iztaccihuatl as she "slept." Now, whenever he thinks about Iztaccihuatl, Popocatépetl shakes and spews ash and smoke.

Myths Surrounding the Ring of Fire

The Ring of Fire contains the greatest number of volcanoes on Earth, and over time people have created many stories about the amazingly explosive region.

In Japan, the most famous volcano is Mount Fuji. According to one myth, this is how Mount Fuji became a volcano: A woman who was really a goddess decided to return to Mount Fuji to live. She knew her husband would miss her, so she left a mirror behind for him to see her in it. Instead of staying behind in his village, he decided to follow her. When he reached the mountain, he looked for his wife everywhere, but when he couldn't find her, he threw himself into the mountain. His mirror caught fire and sent smoke out of the mountain's crater.

In Indonesia, there are many legends about their 125 active volcanoes. One is about the cinder cone volcano, Mount Bromo. In this tale, an ogre wanted to marry a princess. In order to win her hand, he was ordered by the king to dig a trench using half a coconut shell as a shovel. The poor ogre died of exhaustion before he could complete the task. His coconut shell became the cinder cone volcano Mount Bromo.

On Russia's eastern Kamchatka Peninsula, there are 160 volcanoes, 29 of which are currently active. That's the highest number of active

HOW TO STAY SAFE DURING A VOLCANIC ERUPTION

HUNDREDS OF YEARS AGO, people had few tools for protecting themselves against eruptions. Even today, some volcanoes are so unpredictable that the people living nearby can be surprised when they explode. But there are a few ways to stay safe if a volcano blows:

KEEP AWAY FROM LAVA FLOWS. Even if they look solid, they can be red hot inside.

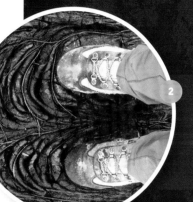

NEVER HIKE BAREFOOT UP A VOLCANIC MOUNTAIN. The solidified lava can be as sharp as glass. And if you have to run because of an unexpected blast, you'll want to be wearing sturdy shoes.

If you're hiking in a volcanic region, **STAY ON THE MARKED TRAIL.** There can be mud pots and lava flows in off-trail areas.

If you're in a town near an eruption, **STAY INDOORS** with the windows closed to keep out ash and lava.

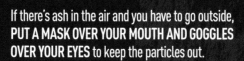

If there's ash in the air and you have to go outside, **PUT A MASK OVER YOUR MOUTH AND GOGGLES OVER YOUR EYES** to keep the particles out.

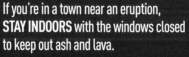

DON'T GO NEAR THE AREAS AFFECTED by the eruption until authorities give the all clear.

SURVIVAL STORY

VOLCANOLOGISTS STUDY VOLCANOES to understand how—and even more importantly *when*—they might erupt. But even the experts can be tricked into believing a volcano is safe when it's not. This happened to Dr. Stanley Williams in 1993. He's a volcanologist from Arizona State University. He was one of a team of 13 scientists studying a volcano called Galeras in Colombia. They were trying to learn its secrets, so they'd be able to warn nearby villagers when it might erupt. Then ... it erupted!

Gas trapped inside the volcano's magma exploded out of its vents. It shot lava bombs and fire through the air. Flaming rocks sent flying from the explosion broke both Williams's legs. Another large piece of tephra bashed him in the head, and he sustained burns all over his body. He was able to crawl partway down the mountain and wedge himself behind a boulder away from the flowing lava. Finally help reached him. Two of his fellow scientists carried him to safety.

Though this was a terrible ordeal, some good came out of it. Using what he'd learned that day, Williams was able to predict Galeras's next eruption, which happened just a few months later. This experience also brought attention to the need for safety precautions in the field—neither Williams nor the other scientists were wearing helmets that day, which could have prevented some of the injuries.

DR. STANLEY WILLIAMS, WHO SURVIVED AN ERUPTION OF GALERAS

volcanoes per square mile anywhere on Earth. In 2013, four of them erupted at the same time! Some of the ethnic groups on the peninsula have legends to explain all the volcanic activity. The Itelmen people of the southern part of the peninsula believed that volcanic eruptions happened when demons flew out of the mountains to hunt for fish. The Koryak people of the northern peninsula believed that the world was created when a Great Raven dropped a feather, which sprang up into the land they call home. The Great Raven created men next, then a woman who was so beautiful that all the men fell in love with her. As the men eventually died, they turned into mountains, each of which burned with love for the woman.

Myths From Ancient Greece and Rome

Like many cultures, the ancient Greeks and Romans turned to their gods to explain why volcanoes erupted. Here are some of their stories.

The Roman god of fire was Vulcan. He was a blacksmith who kept a workshop underground, where he made weapons for the other gods. The pounding of Vulcan's tools made the earth shake. Sometimes, though, Vulcan got really angry—usually at his wife, Venus, the goddess of love. When this happened, he would work so furiously at his forge that smoke and flames would shoot out of the chimneys that rose up from Vulcan's underground workshop to the surface above.

A PAINTING OF SANTORINI ERUPTING IN 1866

The Greek god of fire, Hephaestus, created a bronze giant called Talos to protect the island of Crete from invaders. Talos stood on top of a nearby mountain—possibly on the volcanic island of Thera—and made himself red hot and threw rocks at anyone who approached. According to the myth, a spell was cast on Talos, giving him bad eyesight and causing him to slip. In the fall, all his blood leaked out of him to become lava.

Another Greek myth tells the story of the city of Atlantis. The people of this city were so corrupt that one night the gods destroyed it with earthquakes and fire. It sank into the ocean, never to be seen again. For a long time, people thought this myth was just that—a made-up story. Recently, though, some researchers have noticed that the story shares a lot of similarities with accounts of a huge volcanic eruption that happened in the Aegean Sea. In that account, the ancient Minoan civilization was wiped out when a volcano on what is now the island of Santorini blew up.

Were Atlantis and Santorini the same place? Researchers studying the ancient civilizations have started to find evidence that they may have been.

ANCIENT BRONZE STATUE OF HEPHAESTUS

A MAASAI CHILD AND MOM WITH OL DOINYO LENGAI IN THE DISTANCE

LAVA FROM KĪLAUEA FLOWS OVER A HIGHWAY IN HAWAII.

ICELANDIC VILLAGE BURIED IN ASH AFTER HEKLA ERUPTION

Living in the Volcano's Shadow

The study of volcanoes has progressed a lot since the days of the ancient Greeks and Romans. We went from creating stories and myths to explain their activity to using science to understand why and when volcanoes erupt and the different ways they shape our planet.

But even with all the knowledge we've gained, volcanoes still affect the lives of millions of people around the world. Here's a look at what it's like to live in the shadow of a volcano.

The Downside

It can be dangerous to live close to a volcano if it erupts. Ash, mud, and other volcanic matter can bury hillsides and nearby towns, damaging or destroying homes and crops. The debris can clog rivers and streams and lead to floods. Burning lava can set fire to things in its path, and noxious gases can make it hard for people and animals for miles around to breathe.

The impact of an eruption can be felt even miles away from a volcano. Sometimes those effects are felt for a very long time. Here's a real-life story of a volcano's destruction.

In the year 536, and then again in 540, two supervolcanoes erupted. It happened so long ago that scientists aren't sure which supervolcanoes, but they think one may have been Ilopango in El Salvador.

Soon after the first eruption, writers and historians around the world started documenting some startling changes. In Ireland, wheat for bread wouldn't grow. In China, yellow dust fell "like snow" all over the land. Over most of the Middle East and parts of Europe, fog blocked out the sun. In Scandinavia, temperatures dropped by about 3.6°F (about 2°C), leading to a very long, cold winter. And in Peru, severe drought brought down a once powerful civilization called the

Moche. Across the globe, people froze, starved, and succumbed to plague. Some 25 million people died the year following the first eruption. The number would eventually double, partly because of the second large eruption in 540.

In 1883, when the stratovolcano Krakatau erupted in Indonesia, it not only devastated the land directly around it—two-thirds of the island collapsed into the sea—but it also affected the sea itself. Krakatau's multiple explosions caused huge pyroclastic flows. When these poured into the ocean, they generated a whopping 18 tsunamis. The tsunamis' waves reached heights of 130 feet (39.6 m) as they traveled across the Indian Ocean. They wiped out villages in the nearby islands of Sumatra and Java, and anywhere else they came crashing down. In fact, 165 villages were destroyed in just a single day. Some islands were completely submerged by the waves. In the Thousand Islands off Jakarta's coast, more than 50 miles (80.5 km) distant, people had to climb trees to keep from being washed away.

The tsunami was so powerful, its waves reached all the way to New Zealand and Hawaii. According to at least one researcher, tidal gauges as far away as the British Isles recorded changes believed to be a result of the tsunamis' waves.

You might know about—or even remember—a much more recent eruption that happened in 2010, when the Icelandic volcano Eyjafjallajökull (pronounced ay-yaf-yat-la-YER-kuh-tul) blew. At first its eruptions were nothing unusual for this volcano, just some lava oozing out of a vent in one part of its rocky surface.

But Eyjafjallajökull is a stratovolcano that sits underneath a glacier. When lava started to

SURVIVAL STORY

IN 1992, FILMMAKERS MICHAEL BENSON AND CHRIS DUDDY were filming the bubbling crater of Kīlauea, from a helicopter. Suddenly the helicopter lost power. Benson and Duddy, along with the pilot, Craig Hosking, crashed. The helicopter landed on the crater floor, right next to a boiling-hot pool of lava.

Hosking was able to climb to the top of the crater and into a rescue helicopter, but Benson and Duddy couldn't climb out. The walls of the crater were hot and crumbly. They couldn't see because of thick clouds of sulfur dioxide gas. The gas was so thick, they couldn't even see each other. Neither knew whether his companions were still alive. After spending one night inside the crater, Duddy managed to climb out to safety. Wedged into a crevice, Benson tried to muster the strength to climb out, too. He later recounted that as he struggled to survive, he had visions of the fire goddess Pele coming for him. After two days without food or water, the volcanic fog finally broke. Benson was spotted by a rescue helicopter and was lifted out to safety.

THE BUBBLING CRATER OF KĪLAUEA

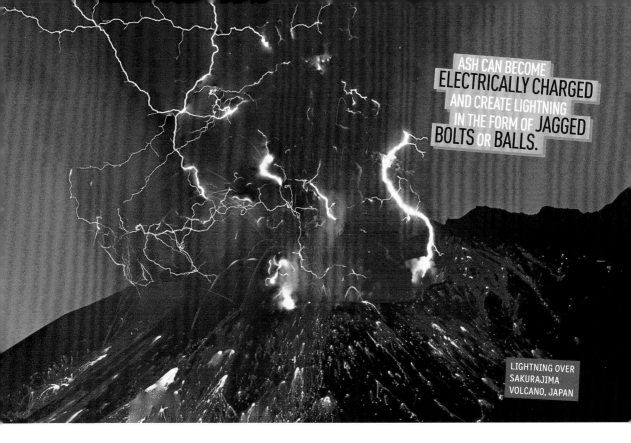

ASH CAN BECOME **ELECTRICALLY CHARGED** AND CREATE LIGHTNING IN THE FORM OF **JAGGED** **BOLTS** OR **BALLS.**

LIGHTNING OVER SAKURAJIMA VOLCANO, JAPAN

pour out of the iced-over vents, the ice melted and turned into steam. Then the steam exploded. Lava came shooting out of the volcano fast and furious. It then cooled so quickly, it shattered into minuscule knife-sharp shards of ash. A plume of this ash rose to a height of 30,000 feet (9,144 m). Made partly of poisonous gases, it was dangerous to breathe. It was also dangerous for planes to fly through the thick ash because it became hard to see out of the cockpit. Even more dangerous for the planes was that the ash could get inside the engines, melt, and stick to the engine parts, making them stall and possibly cause the planes to crash.

A HORSE BEING HERDED TO SAFETY FROM THE ASH OF ICELAND'S EYJAFJALLAJÖKULL IN 2010

The ash from Eyjafjallajökull clogged the skies over the European continent for seven days. That meant most airports there had to shut down. The closures affected travel plans of 10 million people across the globe. But it kept people safe.

It's clear from these volcanic events that eruptions can cause all kinds of things to happen. One of the most interesting effects comes from volcanic ash. Ash and sulfur dioxide that get trapped in the atmosphere can make breathing difficult and dangerous. They can also make sunsets look purple, bright red, or green! As we learned earlier, ash can become electrically charged and create lightning. Some of this lightning can be in the form of jagged bolts. It can also be in the shape of balls. Ball lightning, also called St. Elmo's fire, is mysterious even to scientists. It can roll and also

SURVIVAL STORY

IN 2015, HIKER JEFF BRYDON WAS CAMPING out with his friend Aviv Bromberg on the Villarrica Traverse in Chile. It is a trail that leads past three volcanoes, including Volcán Calbuco. This volcano hadn't erupted in 43 years. When Brydon and Bromberg woke in their tent one morning, it looked as though the sun hadn't risen. Ash clogged the air! Brydon realized Volcán Calbuco had erupted. But which way should they go to escape it? They couldn't see anything! Using their shirts as masks to keep from breathing ash, Brydon and Bromberg set out in the dark to find a trail marker.

After stumbling around, lost and panicked, Bromberg remembered he had a compass. He used it to get back on course. Little by little, they were able to make their way six miles (9.7 km) back down the trail, occasionally being hit by burning ash. Many hours later, they made it to the main road and to safety.

JEFF BRYDON SURVIVED CALBUCO'S 2015 ERUPTION.

bounce off the ground! Because ash attracts water droplets from the air, an eruption can make it rain—or even snow.

The Upside

Though they can cause destruction, there are also benefits volcanoes provide to the people and land around them. Their heat can be used for electricity, and the rocks and minerals they bring up from deep inside Earth's mantle can be used to make all kinds of amazing things—from durable road surfaces to beautiful jewelry. Their cooled lava creates habitats for many kinds of animals and plants and provides rich nutrients to the soil so that all kinds of crops can grow.

Basalt, often found in lava, can be crushed

AT LEAST ONE *MOAI* IS MADE FROM BASALT.

and used to pave roads and parking lots. It's also one of the ingredients in concrete. It can be polished and used to make floor tiles and can also be carved. At least one of the giant *moai*—or "ancestor"—head carvings lined up on the shore of Easter Island in the south Pacific Ocean is made out of basalt.

A thousand years ago, in the region of Lalibela in Ethiopia, there were very few building materials, but residents figured out that they could build their churches by carving them out of basaltic lava deposits. In Cappadocia, Turkey, people have created houses by hollowing out cone-shaped mounds of soft volcanic rock called tuff.

Another kind of volcanic rock, obsidian, has been used to create some useful tools. Obsidian

OBSIDIAN BOULDERS AT THE NEWBERRY NATIONAL VOLCANIC MONUMENT IN OREGON

is a kind of supershiny, glass-like rock that forms when lava cools quickly. When carved, it chips away in flakes. Since the Stone Age (6000 to 2000 B.C.), it has been used to make knives, arrowheads, different kinds of weapons, and other tools. It has also been made into jewelry, mirrors, and figurines. Obsidian objects created hundreds of years ago have been found all over Central America. This rock can be sharpened to such a fine point that it is still used today to make scalpels, tools that doctors use to perform surgery.

Pumice is a lightweight rock that's made when quick-cooling lava is frothy and filled with lots of gas bubbles. Sometimes pumice is ejected into the ocean. Because it floats, it can hang around on top of the waves in large sheets, making it dangerous to passing ships. But pumice also has a lot of uses. Because it's abrasive—rough,

like sandpaper—it turns up in cleansers, face scrubs, and toothpaste. Use a pencil eraser? It's got pumice in it, too. Got a cat? Its litter is probably made of pumice. Wear stonewashed jeans? The stones they were washed with are pumice.

Volcanoes also play a role in our love of gemstones. Perhaps the most coveted of them all is the diamond. It's created when an incredibly high amount of heat and pressure is applied to carbon, changing its structure into a rock that can be cut and polished into a jewel worth thousands of dollars. Diamonds are made deep inside Earth's mantle. They are brought to the surface in rare volcanic rocks called kimberlite. Why are kimberlite rocks so rare? Because they are only brought to the surface in a type of volcanic explosion called a kimberlite eruption, which is also very uncommon. Scientists estimate that we haven't had a kimberlite eruption on our planet in at least 25 million years.

A DIAMOND IN THE ROCK

A DIAMOND IN KIMBERLITE

CONE-SHAPED FORMATIONS IN NEW MEXICO, MADE OF PUMICE AND ASH

THAT'S PHYTOPLANKTON BLOOMING.

A NASA SATELLITE IMAGE OF PHYTOPLANKTON OFF OF WESTERN ICELAND

Volcanoes Can Be Good for Your Health—and Your Garden!

Volcanoes churn up all sorts of useful elements from the center of Earth, like zinc, lead, iron, copper, and gold. People use special tools to mine these elements straight out of volcanic rocks. Rocks and ash from lava flows can also contain a lot of other elements, like potassium and nitrogen, which fertilize soil and make it good for growing crops. Though it can take many years for the ash and lava to break down enough to act as fertilizer, once it does, it seeps deep into the soil, making it nutrient rich and perfect for growing citrus, grapes, olives, all kinds of beans, and many other fruits, vegetables, and flowers. On Mount Merapi in

FERTILE VOLCANIC SOIL IN BALI HELPS RICE GROW.

Indonesia, farmers plant crops, like cauliflower, all the way up the sides of the volcano.

Ash from volcanoes can also be good for the oceans. The iron in volcanic ash can help tiny ocean plants called phytoplankton bloom. And phytoplankton "eats" carbon dioxide, a gas that in high concentration leads to climate change. Phytoplankton is then eaten by small organisms that live in the ocean, at the bottom of the food chain. The small organisms are eaten by bigger fish, all the way up to the biggest creatures in the ocean, such as whales and sharks.

Heat from volcanoes can be turned into geothermal energy for heating our houses. Iceland has about 200 volcanoes, many of which are active. There's so much volcanic activity in Iceland that the country gets more than 25 percent of its

VOLCANIC MUD BATHS

ARIANNA SOLDATI

I KNOW A LOT OF PEOPLE LOVE TO SIT IN VOLCANIC MUD BATHS, and when I was doing fieldwork at Vulcano, I discovered that this was definitely true in this part of Italy. Vulcano is right on the coast, so people sit in this really big mud pool for a while, then take a dip in the sea. The mud baths are always really busy, with lots of people mud bathing. Some believe the sulfur in the mud helps clean your skin. I went down to the baths once and stuck my toe in. It was soft and warm, so that part of it seemed nice. But sulfur stinks like rotten eggs. It's really hard to get the smell out of your clothes, and it takes days to get the smell out of your hair. I didn't want to smell like rotten eggs for days, so I decided not to go all the way in.

HEATED BY VOLCANOES: GEOTHERMAL POWER PLANT, CALIFORNIA

electricity, and 75 percent of its heat and hot water, from geothermal energy—heat that comes up from the ground. This kind of environmentally friendly energy is used in many other countries, including Italy, Indonesia, Japan, and New Zealand. It's used in the United States, too. The Geysers in Northern California is the biggest geothermal field in the world.

Geothermal energy also has other uses, like cooking. In Japan, *kuro-tamago* eggs are a delicacy from Ōwakudani. This region sits inside a caldera that was formed after Mount Hakone erupted 3,000 years ago. The eggs are boiled for an hour inside the sulfur-rich mineral hot springs that are scattered throughout the caldera. While the heat cooks the eggs, the sulfur reacts with the calcium in the eggshells and turns them black. It might be just a myth, but some people consider eggs cooked in sulfur to be extrahealthy. Some legends even say that eating kuro-tamago eggs can add seven years to your life.

In Iceland, rye bread is traditionally prepared by burying the dough and using the thermal heat

VOLCANIC MUD BATHS, AEOLIAN ISLANDS, SICILY

COOKING *KURO-TAMAGO* IN VOLCANICALLY HOT WATER

SNOW MONKEYS RELAXING IN ONSEN HOT SPRINGS, JAPAN

to bake it—sort of like an underground volcano oven! There's also a restaurant outside the capital city of Reykjavík where whole meals are made this way—including fish and vegetables and even cake. In São Miguel, an island in Portugal, a traditional stew is mixed up in a pot and cooked for seven hours using the underground heat from the island's volcanoes. The stew has a little bit of everything in it: pork, beef, chicken, sweet potatoes, cabbage, carrots—and a lot of volcanic heat.

At a restaurant on the Spanish island of Lanzarote, volcanic smoke and steam are used for cooking. The chef there has built a special grill that sits over a vent in the local volcano. Luckily, that volcano has been dormant since 1824.

Volcanoes can also be part of a beauty regimen! Volcanic mud is warm and rich in minerals, and people travel great distances to sit in steaming mud baths.

Other volcanoes create hot springs, which humans (and sometimes monkeys!) use as all-natural hot tubs. In Japan, Sakurajima heats nearby water that people come to soak in. It also heats the nearby sandy beach. It's believed that the warm sand is a cure for achy joints.

FLAMINGOS IN LAKE BOGORIA, KENYA

Volcanoes Are Good for Animals, Too

In a volcanic valley in Kenya, Lake Bogoria is kept warm by geysers. It's also chock-full of minerals like sodium and carbonate. These minerals feed all kinds of algae, which feed crabs, which in turn feed the thousands of pink flamingos that hang out at the lake. Flamingos get their pink coloring from eating food with carotene in it, found in the algae and small crustaceans they eat.

Other animals benefit from volcanoes in different ways. Maleo birds from Indonesia use the heat in the ground to solve a big problem. The maleo is a medium-size bird, but it lays enormous eggs that are actually too big for the birds to sit on to keep them warm. How do they solve this problem? They bury their eggs in the warm soil near the volcanoes. The soil incubates the eggs until they are ready to hatch. Another interesting thing about maleo birds is that their babies hatch already able to

MALEO BIRDS BURY THEIR EGGS IN VOLCANO-HEATED SOIL.

fly—which could come in handy if the volcano starts to blow!

In the Samoan Islands in the south Pacific Ocean, scientists have found what they call an Eel City—hundreds of squirmy eels living near a brand-new underwater volcano called Nafanua. In the Solomon Islands, also in the south Pacific, a group of researchers got a big surprise when they were studying an active volcano there. They found a very rare Pacific sleeper shark living right inside the Kavachi volcano! Why was it there, and how does it survive? No one knows for sure. But scientists are trying to figure it out.

VOLCANO PAINTINGS

ARIANNA SOLDATI

I STARTED MAKING PAINTINGS OF VOLCANOES a few years ago. I did the first one when my boyfriend—who is also a volcanologist—was doing fieldwork in the Aleutian Islands off the coast of Alaska. He was sampling lava and tephra from different volcanoes and was in such a remote area that we couldn't call or email each other. To feel connected to what he was doing, I went online and looked up a picture of Buldir—the volcano he was supposed to visit. I painted it, and I discovered that I really enjoy painting. It relaxes me, and it provides a nice break from studying.

Visual observations are also an important part of volcanology. For example, we use them to describe and classify eruptions. How tall was the column? Was lava still incandescent when it erupted? How far did the ash travel? Painting different kinds of volcanic activity from pictures of real eruptions is an excellent way to focus on these details. As I paint, I try to think of these details and to represent them accurately. It's another way to develop my observation skills, and it comes in handy in the field when I have to sketch eruptions I am witnessing in real time.

I try to set aside a couple of hours a month to make new paintings of different volcanoes, with different styles of eruptions. So far, I've made 13—and counting!

ARIANNA'S PAINTING OF KĪLAUEA AT NIGHT

HOW NATURE RECOVERS AFTER AN ERUPTION: 30 YEARS OF MOUNT ST. HELENS

MODERN-DAY VOLCANIC ERUPTIONS can help scientists learn a lot about how eruptions occur. They can also show how life slowly but surely goes back to normal over the course of many years. Scientists got a good opportunity to study an eruption and its aftermath in the western United States.

On May 18, 1980, Mount St. Helens in Washington State erupted. People had been expecting it to blow for a couple of months. They'd felt the earthquakes trembling under their feet and had watched the mountain puff with steam. But they did not know that this eruption would prove to be one of the most destructive ever. It even rivaled the eruption of Mount Vesuvius, which buried Pompeii in southern Italy in the year A.D. 79.

The eruption of Mount St. Helens killed 57 people and huge numbers of animals. It flattened 200 square miles (518 square km) of forest. It polluted waterways with mud and ash. But in the years since the eruption happened, it has provided scientists of all kinds—volcanologists, ecologists, geologists, and botanists—with amazing insights into what makes a volcano erupt and also how the land, the animals, and the plants around it recover afterward.

Before It Blew

IT WAS A CHILLY MAY DAY in the Pacific Northwest. There was still a little snow on the ground and some ice on top of Spirit Lake. Spring was on the way for the red alder trees, the silver and Douglas firs, and the mountain hemlocks. It was coming for the trout under the lake ice and for the elk, frogs, mountain goats, and

MOUNT ST. HELENS BEFORE IT BLEW IN 1980

gophers that lived inside Gifford Pinchot National Forest, around Mount St. Helens.

People were going about their daily routines this early morning in the Cascade Mountains. Families were camping out. Loggers were chopping trees. Miners were collecting minerals. Geologists were studying the volcanoes in the mountain range: Mount Rainier, Mount Adams, and Mount Hood. But they were especially interested in Mount St. Helens, the youngest mountain in the Cascades, and wondering when it was going to explode.

The last time this 40,000-year-old stratovolcano had erupted was in 1857 (although some scientists think there may have been some smaller eruptions in 1898, 1903, and 1921). Then, in March 1980, hundreds of small earthquakes started rumbling. On March 27, the mountain let off a big blast of steam through its ice-covered crater. The crater began to crack. A week later, it was noticeably bigger and had grown two new cracks. Steam blasted out of it once every hour, then slowed down to once per day. One side of the mountain started to bulge with magma. All signs pointed to an eruption about to happen.

Even so, not everyone was convinced the upcoming blast would be powerful. Despite the scientists' warnings, many people were surprised by what Mount St. Helens had in store.

When the Mountain Exploded

THE FIRST SIGN OF ERUPTION was an earthquake at 8:32 a.m. on Sunday, May 18, 1980. It set off an avalanche of dirt, rocks, and ice that slid down the north face of the mountain and into the valley below. It was the largest debris avalanche ever to happen on Earth, with enough debris to fill one million Olympic-size swimming pools. The avalanche also sliced off the dome of magma that had been building up inside the volcano. All the pressure that had been building for two months was suddenly released. And then, Mount St. Helens exploded—sideways, right

TOUTLE, WASHINGTON, AFTER THE ERUPTION

through the avalanche, which now started to slide at 300 miles an hour (483 km/h) . Adding to the debris was rock and dirt from the volcano's cone, 1,300 feet (396 m) of which had been blasted right off. A few minutes later, there was an explosion of tephra, which reached 15 miles (24.1 km) into the air.

An hour later, Mount St. Helens let out a Plinian-style blast from its vent. More tephra shot out. Pyroclastic flows burst out of the crater, moving at 80 miles an hour (129 km/h). Strong winds spread ash for miles—as far as the Great Plains, 930 miles (1,497 km) away in the midwestern U.S. It created total darkness in the city of Spokane, Washington, 250 miles (402 km) away. Heat from lava and tephra melted snow and ice on the mountain and created massive lahars. They destroyed everything in their path: trees, roads, bridges, and homes. The eruption went on for nine hours.

By the time it was over, life was devastated around the volcano. In a six-mile (9.6-km) ring around Mount St. Helens, all the trees were knocked down and burned. Once pristine lakes and rivers were clogged with dirt and debris. An estimated 7,000 large animals such as deer, elk, and bears were killed. Many birds and small mammals and millions of fish were also killed. Houses and roads could be repaired or rebuilt. But would the natural world around Mount St. Helens ever recover?

MOUNT ST. HELENS'S ERUPTION CAUSED PYROCLASTIC FLOWS

Nature Rebuilds Itself: The Years After the Eruption

MOUNT ST. HELENS EXPLODED multiple times in 1986. It was active again from 1989 to 2001 and from 2004 to 2008. These smaller eruptions created ash, lahars, and pyroclastic flows, but they were nothing like that eruption in May 1980. The world inside Gifford Pinchot National Forest, the area that surrounds the volcano, began its long road to recovery.

SPIRIT LAKE SOON AFTER
MOUNT ST. HELENS ERUPTED

SPIRIT LAKE
30 YEARS LATER!

Nature is resilient. Ten days after the blast, scientists found fungi spreading over the area. Fungi are what help nature rebuild itself after catastrophes like forest fires and volcanic eruptions. They break down decomposing matter that's been left behind, so new things can grow.

Small burrowing animals like mice largely survived the blast, because they were below ground level when it happened. So did some patches of herbs, shrubs, and tree saplings, many of which were protected by the snow that was still on the ground.

After the blast, Spirit Lake went from crystal clear to nearly black from the debris that was dumped into it. For several years it was so dirty, only bacteria could live in it. But as it cleared little by little, sunlight could reach deeper into the water. This helped new plants grow, which brought back fish like trout. Scientists discovered new trout living in the lake in 1993.

LUPINES NOW GROW IN THE ASH AND LAVA LEFT BEHIND.

Debris avalanches created dents in the ground. These dents eventually filled with groundwater and rainwater, making 150 new ponds. One year after the eruption, scientists found tree frogs and western toads living in these ponds. Nine years later, salamanders had returned, too.

Winds blew in spiders and insects, and seeds from lupine flowers, which first sprouted in the area in 1982. Lupines have a lot of nitrogen in them, so they helped restore the nutrients in the soil, which allowed other plants to grow. Gophers helped too. Many of them survived the blast because, like the mice, they were living deep underground. Their tunneling helped mix old dirt and new volcanic ash to make nutrient-rich soil. Elk moved in from surrounding areas, eating plants and pooping out seeds that would grow into new plants.

The 1980 eruption had been devastating, but nature knew exactly what to do to bounce back. Scientists watched and learned. Everything they saw helped them understand how nature recovers from devastating eruptions. Scientists who had studied Mount St. Helens were able to impart their experiences about collecting data and to organize and share information with scientists in other places, such as those who were studying eruptions of the Kasatochi volcano in the Bering Sea, which erupted in 2008, and the Chaitén volcano in Chile, which erupted in 2009.

SUPERWEIRD VOLCANOES AND VOLCANIC FEATURES

THE MORE SCIENTISTS LEARN ABOUT VOLCANOES, the more they discover they still have to learn. Why? Because volcanoes can behave in weird ways. Here are some of the strangest volcanic happenings in the world.

SEISMIC SCREAM

"SCREAMING" VOLCANO REDOUBT, IN ANCHORAGE, ALASKA

WHAT DOES IT MEAN WHEN you hear a mountain screeching like a boiling teakettle? It's a volcano about to blow! In 2009, Redoubt volcano in Alaska erupted. When it did, it made a surprising, high-pitched sound. Turns out that sound was caused by a bunch of tiny earthquakes happening at a rate of 30 per second right under Redoubt's vent. These earthquakes caused what scientists call a seismic scream.

DISAPPEARING ACT

THIS MUD ISLAND APPEARED IN PAKISTAN ... THEN SANK AWAY.

HELLO, VOLCANO ... AND GOODBYE. In 2013, Pakistan was hit by a major 7.7-magnitude earthquake. Soon after, an island that was named Zalzala Koh poked out of the water in the Arabian Sea. But the small, 300-by-120-foot (91.4-by-36.6-m) island was actually a mud volcano that formed when movement from the earthquake caused liquid under the seafloor to expand. Mud pushed up and *voilà!* An island! By 2016, the sea eroded the mud and Zalzala Koh was gone.

COLORFUL ERUPTIONS

KAWAH IJEN'S BLUE SULFUR FLAMES

RED ISN'T THE ONLY HOT VOLCANO COLOR. When Kawah Ijen volcano on the island of Java in Indonesia erupts, it sends blue flames down the side of its mountain. The color comes from the really hot sulfur gas catching fire when it comes in contact with oxygen. The blue gas condenses into liquid. When the liquid cools and hardens, it turns into a powdery yellow mineral that is scattered all over the crater floor.

SHATTERING LAVA

OL DOINYO LENGAI'S CARBONATITE LAVA FOUNTAIN, HARDENED IN MIDAIR

ALTHOUGH ALL A'A LAVA HAS A GLASSY QUALITY, the lava that comes out of Ol Doinyo Lengai in Tanzania takes it to the next level. Its lava is really runny—like olive oil. When the lava droplets cool, they hit the ground and shatter like glass.

GET IN THE FLOW!

ERUPTING VOLCANOES AREN'T THE ONLY NATURAL DISASTERS that can occur on our planet. Different parts of the planet are also susceptible to hurricanes, tornadoes, earthquakes, and wildfires. Each of these events may require us to leave our homes in order to stay safe.

Work with your family to come up with your own **FAMILY EMERGENCY EVACUATION PLAN** (**FEEP**).

MAKE YOUR OWN FEEP

You'll need to figure out:

☑ What are the types of natural disasters common in your region?

☑ Find out what the emergency, evacuation, and shelter plans are in your community.

☑ Where can you stay for a few days if you have to leave your town or city? Find out if you have family members who live within driving distance or if there are hotels or motels outside the danger area. If you have animals, make sure they allow pets.

☑ If you can't drive, what other means of transportation are available? Buses? Ferries? Trains?

☑ How will you and your family members find each other if you're separated? Work with your family to pick a meeting place. It can be your home, the home of a friend or relative, or your school.

EMERGENCY EVACUATION PLAN

Section 1: General Guidelines

Available Exits:

Meeting Place:

Equipment:

FIND MORE information about putting together a Family Emergency Evacuation Plan at **ready.gov**.

Assemble supplies, including:

NONPERISHABLE FOOD TO LAST THREE DAYS

MONEY AND IDENTIFICATION

BOTTLED WATER TO LAST THREE DAYS

MAPS

A FIRST AID KIT

A BATTERY-OPERATED RADIO, FOR LISTENING TO WEATHER AND EVACUATION UPDATES

PRESCRIPTION MEDICATION

PET FOOD

EXTRA GAS FOR THE CAR

FLASHLIGHT AND EXTRA BATTERIES

VOLCANOLOGISTS STUDYING
PITON DE LA FOURNAISE,
RÉUNION ISLAND

CHAPTER 4

SERIOUS
SCIENCE

INTRODUCTION

VULCANO IS AN ISLAND IN ITALY, JUST NORTH OF SICILY.

When I was 22 years old, I spent two weeks volunteering at the Vulcano observatory. My job was to explain the volcano and its dangers to visitors.

ARIANNA SOLDATI

I was supervised by a volcanologist, whose main research had to do with gas measurements.

I got up at 4 a.m. the first time I climbed Vulcano. If I had tried to climb the volcano after my volunteer shift was over at 6 p.m., the temperature outside would have been too hot. The smell of sulfur from the fumaroles (that's what we call vents around the volcano that release gas and steam) was really strong, like rotten eggs. The gas irritated my throat and I coughed a lot. The terrain changed beneath my feet as I climbed, going from soft soil to hard rock. By the time I got to the top, the sun was rising. It was amazing to be up there—very quiet and incredibly peaceful. There's no vegetation, so it was like being in a high desert. I could look

out and see the neighboring islands and their volcanoes and, in the distance, the lights of cities and towns.

Vulcano has a lot of spectacular gas activity, but the first time I saw Vulcano, there was a lot more gas coming out of its fumaroles than usual. Increased gas activity doesn't necessarily mean an eruption is going to happen. A lot of the gas escaping from fumaroles is water vapor, so the activity might simply be related to how much it's rained.

More telling are the yellow sulfur deposits around Vulcano's fumaroles. Different gases come out from different depths. Sulfur comes from magma, which is usually deep inside Earth's mantle. All volcanoes release gas, but if you see lots of sulfur deposits, you know the magma is near the surface. When I got a whiff of that rotten-egg smell, it probably meant sulfur gases from the magma below were producing that odor. And later, when I looked inside the volcano's heart-shaped crater, I realized I had been observing firsthand that this volcano was a living, changing thing.

THE YELLOW CRYSTALS ARE SULFUR.

ALL THAT SULFUR CAN MAKE FOR ONE SMELLY VOLCANO!

DIFFERENT GASES COME FROM DIFFERENT DEPTHS. SULFUR COMES FROM MAGMA, WHICH IS USUALLY DEEP INSIDE EARTH'S MANTLE.

AL VOLCAN TO THE VOLCANO

VULCANO'S FUMAROLES, SEEN FROM ABOVE

VULCANO DEGASSING

OFTEN, THE STORY OF HUMANS IS ALSO THE STORY OF VOLCANOES.

Our survival depends on our understanding of the explosive forces of the planet we live on (and maybe, one day, other planets, too). And we build our understanding through science.

The word that describes the science of volcanoes is *volcanology*. But volcanology doesn't focus on only one thing. Volcanologists study a lot of different aspects of historic and modern eruptions so they can better predict what might happen in the future. Many volcanologists are geologists—that is, they study how Earth was formed, through its rocks, metals, minerals, water, gases, and oil. Geologists who collect rocks outdoors, or out in the field, are called field geologists.

Physical volcanologists are geologists who study how volcanoes form and function. They also study what comes out of volcanoes when they erupt. This information helps us understand a lot about the history of a volcano, which can also help us understand what it might do in the future.

Geophysicists study the Earth's crust and tectonic plates. Some of their work might involve researching the earthquakes that go along with volcanic eruptions, and how gravity and a planet's magnetic field affect them. Geophysicists might also coordinate with seismologists—scientists who study earthquakes—to understand how the vibrations caused by earthquakes affect volcanoes and the movement of tectonic plates.

Geodesic volcanologists study how a volcano's shape and the area around it change. And geochemists study the composition and chemical aspects of Earth. They also study the chemical makeup of gases, lava, and ash.

There are many more types of scientists whose work includes the study of volcanoes. Working both alone and together in teams, these brave men and women help us understand our

VOLCANOLOGIST OBSERVING AN ERUPTION UP CLOSE AT MOUNT ETNA

SAMPLING LAVA FROM PITON DE LA FOURNAISE, ON RÉUNION ISLAND IN THE INDIAN OCEAN

Earth and help keep us safe from the magma beneath our feet.

Volcano Scientists on the Job

The United States alone has 169 active volcanoes. And 54 of these are considered a threat. That means they could erupt at any time and put people's lives in danger. But volcano scientists are on the job, working hard to predict when these volcanoes might blow! They're studying rocks from previous eruptions and looking at lava, gas, and water from current eruptions. Volcanologists are also studying the shape of volcanoes and making computer models of eruptions, and more—all to help us stay safe living with volcanoes. Here are some of the questions these scientists try to answer: Is it safe to build homes or farms or factories near active or dormant volcanoes? Is it safe for airplanes to fly over a volcano when a volcano is spewing gas and ash? When is it okay to go back home once an eruption has ended?

Volcano scientists keep an eye on volcanoes to determine what the current danger level is and to predict the timing and details of a future eruption. Some of this monitoring happens at volcano observatories. There are five of these in the United States: in Alaska, where most of the active volcanoes are, and also in California, the Cascades region of the Pacific Northwest, Hawaii, and Yellowstone National Park. Each observatory is responsible for monitoring all the active volcanoes in its region. Scientists from geological institutions and universities work together to do this. They also exchange information with organizations like the National Oceanic and Atmospheric Administration, which monitors weather and climate, and keep in touch with volcano-watching organizations in other countries.

What's That Volcano Up To?

Over many years of careful study, volcano scientists now know exactly what to monitor to predict an eruption. First, they check seismic activity—earthquakes. They also look for changes in the ground around a volcano: The ground often swells before an eruption, because of the rising

NASA'S INTERNATIONAL SPACE STATION 5 (ISS-5) MISSION CREW SNAPPED MOUNT ETNA'S ERUPTION PLUME FROM SPACE.

A VOLCANOLOGIST MONITORING GASES AT KĪLAUEA'S PU'U 'Ō'Ō VENT

HOW STRONG WAS IT? MEASURING VOLCANIC BLASTS

THE STRENGTH OF VOLCANIC ERUPTIONS varies, so volcanologists devised a chart called the Volcanic Explosivity Index, or VEI, that rates volcanoes on a scale of 0 to 8. This doesn't mean it couldn't go higher one day—8 is just the highest we know about so far (and thankfully a Category 8 eruption hasn't been recorded in human history).

Below is a definition of each level on the VEI.

VEI 0–2: Small eruptions that happen every day or every week. Mauna Loa in Hawaii has VEI-0–1 eruptions. Unzen in Japan had a VEI-2 eruption in 1792.

VEI 3: Severe eruptions that happen every year. Their eruption plumes are at least 9.32 miles (15 km) long. Nevado del Ruiz in Colombia had a VEI-3 eruption in 1985.

RUSSIA'S SARYCHEV VOLCANO, SEEN ERUPTING FROM SPACE

A POWERFUL ERUPTION OF ANAK KRAKATAU, INDONESIA

VEI 4–5: Massive eruptions that happen every 10–100 years. These eruption plumes are at least 15.5 miles (25 km) long. When Mount Pelée in the Caribbean erupted in 1902, it was VEI 4, and Mount St. Helens's in 1980 was VEI 5.

VEI 6–7: Colossal and supercolossal eruptions like Krakatau (VEI 6, in 1883) and Tambora (VEI 7, in 1815) in Indonesia. These shroud the sky in ash and darkness and create other destructive weather events, like tsunamis.

VEI 8: The level of eruption that a megacolossal supervolcano like Yellowstone would have if it ever blew again. Volcanologists describe the effects of VEI-8 eruptions as "catastrophic"; that's how powerful they could be.

magma. Finally they measure changes in the volcano's temperature and the chemical makeup of gas, water, or lava escaping from it. Sometimes that information is compared to data collected from old eruptions.

It's common for a volcanic eruption to be preceded by earthquakes—that is, as the magma rises, the earth shakes gently with what are called low-frequency earthquakes that only instruments can "feel." Some of these earthquakes are so small, we can't feel them even if we're standing right on top of them. But machines called seismographs can. When a volcano is dormant, scientists place seismographs in and around it. These send signals to machines back at an observatory, where they're read by seismologists. A seismologist can tell what kinds of earthquakes are happening and if they are cause for alarm. Not all earthquakes mean that magma and gas are rising inside a volcano, putting stress on the crust for an eventual BOOM. But closely spaced tremors, especially when they happen in groups called swarms, tell seismologists an eruption may be on the way.

The changes in the earth around or on a volcano are known as deformations. A deformation on a volcano can be a bulge, such as what grew on one side of Mount St. Helens before its 1980 eruption. It can be a crack in a volcano's surface, or the ground sinking around it. Deformations show that magma, gas, and/or water are moving, and maybe pooling up, underneath the volcano. These changes are often too subtle to be noticed with the naked eye, so volcanologists use many tools to monitor deformation.

GPS STATIONS COLLECTING AND TRANSMITTING DATA, IN THREE SISTERS, OREGON

For example, special, supersensitive field instruments called tilt-meters and strainmeters send information back to scientists at the observatory. Tiltmeters are placed in drilled-out holes near a volcano. These instruments measure the slope of the ground around it. Strainmeters are also placed in holes, but they measure the change in distance between two points. Using these two measuring tools, volcanologists can keep track of how the area around a volcano shifts—and whether that shifting may mean an explosion is on the way.

Volcanologists also monitor deformation by using satellite images. With radar, satellites in space take high-resolution pictures of a volcano over time. These pictures feed into a computer program that creates a model of the volcano and the area around it, revealing any changes. This not only helps scientists understand if an eruption is coming but also helps them figure out the shape of the terrain and where lava has flowed in the past. With this information, scientists can understand how lava might move the next time—and where a safe place to set up new monitoring stations might be!

HARRAT KHAYBAR VOLCANO IN SAUDI ARABIA, PHOTOGRAPHED FROM THE INTERNATIONAL SPACE STATION

SAMPLE BOTTLE OF STEAM AND GAS FROM YELLOWSTONE

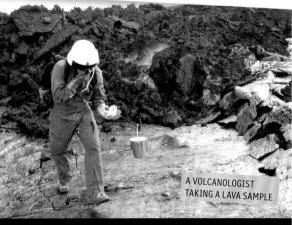

A VOLCANOLOGIST TAKING A LAVA SAMPLE

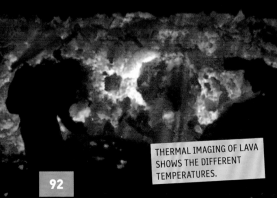

THERMAL IMAGING OF LAVA SHOWS THE DIFFERENT TEMPERATURES.

Now That's Hot!

We already know that things get mighty hot underneath a volcano. But temperatures don't always stay the same down there. The stuff that comes out of volcanoes—the steam that creates mud pots and gas vents, the water that creates geysers and hot springs, and of course lava— changes temperature depending on what's going on inside the mountain. When things really start heating up, the volcano is ready to blow. So volcanologists use devices called thermocouples to measure temperatures. They can place these right on a vent or even on the surface of some slow-moving lava.

Even if they can't get close to a volcano, scientists can still measure heat rising from the ground using a special thermal-imaging camera or using the temperature data sent by satellites in space. Scientists also measure what's in the water and gas coming out of volcanoes. When magma is deep in Earth, it gives off carbon dioxide and water vapor. As it rises, sulfur dioxide is released. So when scientists notice an increase in sulfur dioxide, that's another sign that an eruption is coming.

Volcanologists also get a lot of information from simply watching what a volcano is doing. For example, when viewing all the explosive action from the deck of an observatory, they might record information such as how high an ash plume gets, how long an eruption lasts, and how much lava they think is flowing.

Some volcanologists do get up close—and hands on. They dress in special protective gear and lug lots of equipment up to where all the action happens. Sometimes volcanologists in the field spend several days on active volcanoes, and some note feeling almost choked by the gassy fumes. Some scientists have described having to actually outrun lava flows.

Getting up close to an erupting volcano has

its advantages. Scientists might take samples of volcanic rock or still gooey lava to run tests on them and to compare them to samples from ancient eruptions. They might fly in a helicopter over a bubbling caldera to observe the volcanic activity inside. Sometimes they'll just place monitoring equipment at the volcano to record information, so they can review the data later. They might also explore lava tubes or camp out at a volcano's summit, so they can see how its activity changes from day to day.

Under Water and Outer Space

For a very particular kind of volcanologist, the field is actually the ocean. Submarine volcanologists are a rare type of volcano scientist—there aren't many of them. But what they learn from studying eruptions underwater is important for understanding the geological changes of our planet. Sometimes submarine volcanologists study the size and composition of rafts of air-filled pumice that float to the surface after eruptions. These floating rocks tell scientists more about the power and size of underwater eruptions. One

recent pumice mass was the size of Israel!

Although submarine volcanologists do go on expeditions on ships, they often have to rely on underwater robots to record volcanic activity in places where the pressure and heat are too high for humans to withstand.

Planetary geologists study volcanoes in space. Unfortunately, they aren't able to study those volcanoes in the field—so a lot of their work happens inside an observatory. For example, they use tools like a spectrometer—a tool that measures the wavelengths of light—to watch volcanic activity on Jupiter. Believe it or not, those wavelengths can give scientists a lot of information about the planet—including what a rock is made up of or how hot a gas is—*from millions of miles away!* Planetary volcanologists use the data they get from volcanoes on one planet to help them find volcanoes on other bodies and figure out if those bodies have volcanic activity.

A planetary volcanologist named Rosaly Lopes holds the world record for discovering the most active volcanoes *anywhere*. She's found 71 of them, on Jupiter's moon Io.

PLANETARY GEOLOGISTS STUDY VOLCANOES USING DATA FROM SATELLITES.

A SUBMARINE VOLCANOLOGIST CHECKS OUT THE LAS GEMELAS SEAMOUNT.

WHAT'S IN A VOLCANOLOGIST'S TOOL KIT?

SAMPLE BAGS
FOR COLLECTING LAVA AND ASH

GAS MASK

NOTEBOOKS AND PENCILS

ALUMINUM-COATED HEAT SUIT
THAT CAN WITHSTAND TEMPS UP TO 500°F/260°C IF THEY'RE GOING ALL THE WAY INTO AN ACTIVE CRATER

FLASHLIGHT

LASER RANGE FINDER
TO CALCULATE DISTANCE BETWEEN OBJECTS

SUNSCREEN

WALKIE-TALKIE

WORK GLOVES

FIRST AID KIT

GLOW STICKS
FOR SIGNALING AND MARKING THE POSITION OF OTHERS IN THE GROUP

PICKS
FOR COLLECTING ROCK SAMPLES

CLIMBING ROPES & HELMET
IF THEY'RE EXPECTING FALLING ROCKS OR EXPLODING TEPHRA

MAGNIFYING GLASS

DRILLS AND HAMMERS
FOR MAKING HOLES IN ROCK

FOR LOWERING PEOPLE AND GEAR INTO A CRATER

WATER

TO COOL LAVA SAMPLES

Bring in the Robots!

Sometimes, when volcanologists can't get up close and personal with fiery volcanoes, they send in the bots. That's right: Remote-controlled robots can do some of the hot work for them! One such robot was an eight-legged robot named Dante that was lowered into Mount Erebus in Antarctica—the first nonhuman volcano "scientist." Dante spent a few days getting down to the crater floor and collecting data, then transmitting it to a lab via satellite, before being hoisted out.

Robots can be especially useful to submarine volcanologists, because they can go down into volcanoes' watery vents, where they can watch (and film) ash and pillowy lava erupting. In 2008, volcanologists used remote-controlled weather balloons to take measurements of carbon dioxide and sulfur dioxide puffing out of the mouth of Hawaii's Kīlauea volcano. Robots can take some of the danger out of studying volcanoes, and they can go where people can't. But the observations that humans make by just being at the site still drive many volcanologists to get hands on.

Volcanoes and Climate Change

Our planet is currently getting hotter and hotter because of climate change. This affects how high volcanic gases such as sulfur dioxide climb into the atmosphere. Scientists think that instead of volcanic gases and particles making it all the way to the stratosphere, they're getting caught in a lower layer, called the troposphere. And when those gases and particles get stuck in the troposphere, they don't reach the stratosphere, where they protect us from the heat of the sun. Instead, they rain back down to Earth.

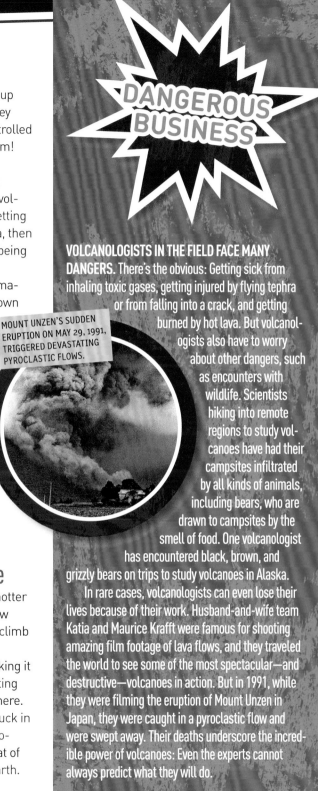

DANGEROUS BUSINESS

MOUNT UNZEN'S SUDDEN ERUPTION ON MAY 29, 1991, TRIGGERED DEVASTATING PYROCLASTIC FLOWS.

VOLCANOLOGISTS IN THE FIELD FACE MANY DANGERS. There's the obvious: Getting sick from inhaling toxic gases, getting injured by flying tephra or from falling into a crack, and getting burned by hot lava. But volcanologists also have to worry about other dangers, such as encounters with wildlife. Scientists hiking into remote regions to study volcanoes have had their campsites infiltrated by all kinds of animals, including bears, who are drawn to campsites by the smell of food. One volcanologist has encountered black, brown, and grizzly bears on trips to study volcanoes in Alaska.

In rare cases, volcanologists can even lose their lives because of their work. Husband-and-wife team Katia and Maurice Krafft were famous for shooting amazing film footage of lava flows, and they traveled the world to see some of the most spectacular—and destructive—volcanoes in action. But in 1991, while they were filming the eruption of Mount Unzen in Japan, they were caught in a pyroclastic flow and were swept away. Their deaths underscore the incredible power of volcanoes: Even the experts cannot always predict what they will do.

That's why volcanoes are another piece of the climate-change puzzle that many scientists around the world are trying to piece together.

Know Your Volcano Alerts

All the information that volcanologists collect from their instruments, observations, and hands-on work goes back to the lab, where it's analyzed by computers and more scientists. When all this data comes together, a picture of a volcano's personality starts to emerge. The better scientists can understand volcanoes, the better they can be about predicting a volcano's eruptions.

So when scientists are pretty sure a volcano will erupt, how do they get the word out? First the folks at volcano observatories create and publish regular status and activity reports for everyone to see. You can actually view these for yourself on observatory web pages, such as the

one the United States Geological Survey (USGS) maintains to monitor volcanoes in the United States. Volcano observatories publish their reports either monthly, weekly, daily, or even hourly, as conditions demand. These reports cover gas emissions, earthquake rumblings, and more. And when a volcano actually erupts, the reports include information about lahars, lava and pyroclastic flows, and how much ash is in the air. Alerts range from normal, when the volcano is quiet, to advisory, when it's starting to get restless, to watch, when it seems like the volcano could blow, but no one's quite sure when.

Next there's the warning alert. A warning is what scientists at an observatory issue if a volcano is about to explode. They alert various government organizations about the risks associated with the eruptions, too. Do people need to be evacuated? If so, how many, and how far away should they go? How much time do people have to get to safety?

ASTRONAUTS ON THE SPACE SHUTTLE *ENDEAVOUR* PHOTOGRAPHED KAMCHATKA'S 60,000-FOOT ASH COLUMN.

ALERT-LEVEL TERMS

When the volcano-alert level is changed, a Volcano Activity Notice (VAN) is issued.

NORMAL	Volcano is in typical background, noneruptive state or, *after a change from a higher level,* volcanic activity has ceased and volcano has returned to noneruptive, background state.
ADVISORY	Volcano is exhibiting signs of elevated unrest above known background level or, *after a change from a higher level,* volcanic activity has decreased significantly but continues to be closely monitored for possible renewed increase.
WATCH	Volcano is exhibiting heightened or escalating unrest with increased potential of eruption, time frame uncertain, **OR** eruption is under way but poses limited hazards.
WARNING	Hazardous eruption is imminent, under way, or suspected.

REAL-TIME ALERTS

EVERY U.S. OBSERVATORY ISSUES REAL-TIME ALERTS for the volcanoes in its region. Here's one from Alaska on May 17, 2017. At 8:48 a.m. on that day, Bogoslof volcano was on a warning alert after an eruption the previous day.

JUST 18 MINUTES INTO BOGOSLOF'S MASSIVE 2017 ERUPTION

ALASKA VOLCANO OBSERVATORY STATUS REPORT
U.S. Geological Survey
Wednesday, May 17, 2017, 12:48 AM AKDT (Wednesday, May 17, 2017, 08:48 UTC)

BOGOSLOF VOLCANO (VNUM #311300)
53°55'38" N 168°2'4" W, Summit Elevation 492 ft (150 m)
Current Volcano Alert Level: WARNING
Current Aviation Color Code: RED

Following the explosive eruption that occurred at 22:32 AKST tonight (06:32 UTC May 17) and lasted about 73 minutes, seismicity and infrasound as detected on neighboring islands has been quiet. The eruption produced an ash cloud that moved southwest along the edge of a mass of weather clouds as seen in satellite images.

Bogoslof volcano remains at a heightened state of unrest and in an unpredictable condition. Additional explosions producing high-altitude volcanic clouds could occur at any time. Low-level explosive activity that is below our ability to detect in our data sources may be occurring. These low-level explosions could pose a hazard in the immediate vicinity of the volcano.

The Aviation Color Code remains at RED and the Alert Level remains at WARNING.

The National Weather Service (NWS) has issued a Marine Weather Statement indicating trace amounts (less than 1 mm) of ashfall are possible in the region from Cape Sarichef to Nikolski.

A SIGMET warning for aviation is in effect for the volcanic cloud at an altitude of 34,000 ft above sea level. Status of the ash cloud forecast can be found at the National Weather Service Alaska Aviation Weather Unit website at http://aawu.arh.noaa.gov/

USGS
science for a changing world

FIREFIGHTERS WORK TO STOP THE LAVA FLOW FROM MOUNT ETNA, ITALY.

COOLING LAVA WITH WATER HOSES

KIDS IN JAPAN USE GOGGLES AND MASKS TO PROTECT THEMSELVES FROM THE ASH FROM MOUNT ASO'S ERUPTION.

Scientists also issue a red code to let aviation professionals at airports and pilots in the air know that an eruption is on the way or under way and that they need to watch out for ash.

Working together, all these various organizations continue to monitor and communicate what's going on at the volcano, make decisions about safety, and decide when it's time to warn people to evacuate or when it's safe for people to go back home.

Sometimes government organizations may work to try to lessen the effects of an exploding volcano. They might build barricades, dig trenches—or even drop bombs—to try to make lava flow away from houses and roads. They might spray the lava with cold water to get it to cool off and stop flowing. Do any of these things actually work? Not really. Lava is so heavy and hot that when there's a big flow, people can't really do much to stop it.

There are a few actions we can take to keep people and property safe from really active volcanoes, though. In volcanically active regions of Japan, school children practice evacuation drills and wear construction hard hats on their way to and from home, to keep them safe from tephra and any other flying debris. The government has also built many concrete shelters along roads and highways, where people can hide out from lava flows until help comes.

Some safety measures are a little more drastic. Governments sometimes decide to create exclusion zones. These are areas close enough to potential lava flows that no one is allowed to live there. The island of Montserrat in the Caribbean has an active volcano called Soufrière Hills. When it erupted in 1995, it wiped out the capital city and buried it in ash. More than half the island is now an exclusion zone, and the capital has been moved to the southern tip of the island.

Our Ever Changing Planet

Every day, volcanoes change the planet we live on. They can leave behind a lot of destruction in their wake, but that destruction can also be a building block for new life! Volcanoes build habitats with their lava flows, for creatures on land and under the ocean. Volcanoes also change the air we breathe and the water in our seas.

NEW SCIENCE

SURE, VOLCANOLOGISTS HAVE SUPERCOOL TOOLS like tilt-meters and satellites for helping them predict eruptions. But newly discovered clues, and new gadgets, might help scientists get even better at understanding volcanoes. Here's a look at THREE COOL NEW TOOLS in the volcanology arsenal:

SCIENTISTS STUDIED VOLCÁN TELICA TO CONFIRM THEIR THEORY OF ABSOLUTE STILLNESS BEFORE ERUPTION.

Most volcanoes show clear signs that they're about to erupt—displaying everything from deformation to extra earthquakes. But some volcanoes are so jittery all the time, it can be hard for scientists to get a read on what's really going on inside them. In 2016, an international team of scientists figured out an important piece of information: Volcanoes have A PERIOD OF ABSOLUTE STILLNESS just before they erupt. The longer that stillness period lasts, the bigger the explosion will be when it finally happens.

In 2006, a team of European and Latin American scientists developed a way to predict eruptions—with their ears. They devised software that could turn a volcano's seismic activity into SOUND WAVES. In scientific terms, they figured out how to *sonify* it. Now scientists can listen to a volcano's "song" to try to understand its seismic patterns.

BEFORE IT BLEW, MOUNT ETNA HAD A PERIOD OF STILLNESS.

Believe it or not, scientists think that in the near future, volcanic activity could be measured by clocks—not just any clock, but superaccurate ATOMIC CLOCKS. These clocks use atomic activity—that's the movement of the electrons and neutrons inside an atom—to keep time. Atomic clocks are the most accurate, precise, and predictable clocks in the world. Researchers think that when magma fills an underground chamber, it may cause clocks placed nearby to tick at a different rate than a clock that's 100 miles (161 km) away. This means that a clock on top of a volcano could give clues that magma is gathering and ready to be released. So far, volcanologists are still researching this idea, and as of October 2017 they've yet to install any atomic clocks in the field.

ATOMIC CLOCKS MIGHT ONE DAY HELP PREDICT ERUPTIONS.

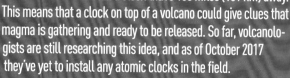

WAIT AROUND FOR A FEW THOUSAND YEARS, AND YOU'LL GET A WHOLE FOREST, COMPLETE WITH ALL THE ANIMALS NATIVE TO THE ENVIRONMENT.

AFTER ERUPTIONS LIKE MOUNT ST. HELENS'S, NEW LIFE FINDS A WAY TO GROW.

In some places, you can actually see these changes happening right before your eyes. This was the case in the Gifford Pinchot National Forest.

There wasn't much left of the surrounding forest when Mount St. Helens finished with it in 1980. But soon after, plants and animals began to return to the area. The regrowth was slow and difficult. And it didn't go back to what residents of Washington State might call "normal." Instead, nature created its own new normal. And ultimately, that's what life on Earth is all about.

We have a name for this new life that comes back to a place that's been destroyed by a volcano. It's called primary succession. This is when an entire ecosystem is wiped out—even its soil—and it's replaced with volcanic rock. In that process, the

FERNS JOIN MOSSES IN TAKING OVER FOR LICHENS.

first things we can see growing on this rock are lichens. Lichens are a kind of half fungi (like mushrooms) and half bacteria or algae. They don't need soil to grow, which is how they're able to live in this extreme environment. The acid they let off helps to break down the volcanic rock and turn it to soil. Dead lichens also break down and add to this mixture.

Fungi might show up soon after an eruption, too, and certain kinds of bacteria. These things are all called pioneer species. They're the first things that move in to help a landscape recover and rebuild its soil.

After several years of lichens turning rock to soil, there's enough soil for mosses to start growing. Mosses add to the rebuilding process and provide a moist home for insects to live. The soil gets deeper over time, and after a while, it's deep enough for

FERNS GROWING OUT OF ROCKS ON KĪLAUEA

LICHENS DON'T NEED SOIL TO GROW AFTER AN ERUPTION.

ferns to grow. As the soil continues to deepen, grasses show up, then wildflowers, then finally shrubs and some small trees. Wait around for a few thousand years, and you'll get a whole forest, complete with all the animals native to the environment.

Hawaii is an extremely volcanic place that's always rebuilding itself. The life that grows in Hawaii is different from the life that grows in Washington State. So the flora, or plant life, that you'll find in these places is different, too. In tropical Hawaii, a very rare plant called silversword grows in the rocky soil at the top of Mauna Kea. But the Hawaiian islands have dry sides, and wet sides where a lot more rain falls. This has an effect on which plants grow and how fast. On the Big Island's dry side, there are almost no grasses growing over the

PAHOEHOE LAVA FLOWING FROM KĪLAUEA. ONE DAY PLANTS MAY GROW HERE.

lava flows that happened hundreds of years ago. On the wet side, there are ferns and small trees growing over two-year-old lava flows.

Volcanic soil can be really good for crops, too. But some planted crops flourish in volcanic soil more than others do. Coffee, grapes, and blueberries all love to tuck their roots into the mineral-rich volcanic soils.

See a Volcano in Action

If volcanoes are changing the world all the time, is it possible to see some of that eruption action? The answer is yes! There are a number of active volcanoes that visitors can observe firsthand. One that might be close to where you live is Kīlauea on Hawaii's Big Island. It sits inside a national park, and it's been oozing out lava since 1983. Visitors can drive around the

FUTURE WORLD

TECTONIC PLATES SHIFT, AND VOLCANOES ERUPT. Over time these two actions will change the surface of our planet. Here are some scientific predictions:

1,000 YEARS: Mount Vesuvius will have erupted 40 times, and Hawaii will have moved 295 feet (89.9 m) to the north and west. Mauna Loa will have erupted 200 times.

10,000 YEARS: Mount Vesuvius will have erupted hundreds of times, enough to fill its caldera, Monte Somma. Hawaii will have moved half a mile (0.8 km) to the north and west, and Kīlauea will be 328 feet (100 m) taller. Nearby, the Lōʻihi Seamount will have risen 656 feet (200 m) higher off the seafloor, but it will still have to grow another 23 feet (7 m) before it reaches the surface of the ocean.

100,000 YEARS: Hawaii will have moved 5.5 miles (8.8 km) to the north and west, which might make Kīlauea and Lōʻihi more active than Mauna Loa. Kīlauea will be more than half a mile (0.8 km) taller, and Lōʻihi Seamount will be well above sea level.

1 MILLION YEARS: Hawaii will have moved 56 miles (90.1 km) to the north and west. Some of the volcanoes in the Cascades mountain range will be extinct or sunken in from caldera collapses. But new volcanoes will have started erupting. We just have no idea where those will be ... yet.

island and see it in action. You can hike in and look at it close up—or camp out and watch its hot, bright lava flows light up the night sky.

On the far side of the Ring of Fire is the volcanic complex of Asosan in Japan. Visitors to this site can walk around its caldera, take a cable car to the top of Mount Nakadake, one of Asosan's five active stratovolcanoes, and visit a volcanically heated hot spring. This volcano last erupted in 2016, but it's being constantly monitored for new activity. Be sure to check reports and alerts before you travel to see it.

Tucked away in the Cordillera de los Maribios mountains in Nicaragua is Cerro Negro. This cinder cone volcano is active but hasn't erupted since 1999. Its lifeless slopes, still covered with black ash from its past eruptions, have inspired a new trend: ash boarding. That's right—people come from all over the world to climb up a 1,600-foot (488-m) volcano, then slide down on a wooden board at speeds that can reach 50 miles an hour (80.5 km/h) . It's like snowboarding or sledding, but on ash instead of snow.

ASH BOARDING DOWN CERRO NEGRO!

Studying Volcanic Land

There might be nothing cooler than seeing a volcano erupting and making new land. But the results of ancient eruptions and seismic shifts can still be found everywhere. You just have to know where to look. Studying these features is like gazing back in time, and imagining how the land was before can be a great mental exercise.

There are two types of rocky volcanic forms found on Earth. The first are extrusive landforms. That is land formed when magma makes it to the surface of the planet in the form of lava and cools.

Examples of extrusive landforms include conical vents, seafloor spread from mid-ocean-ridge eruptions, composite volcanoes with layers of built-up rock, and land made by the Hawaiian volcanoes.

Another example is on the coast of Northern Ireland. A thick wad of blocky columns forms an uneven trail out into the Irish Sea. It's called Giant's Causeway. Legend says that these blocks were laid by a giant named Finn McCool. Science tells us that these slabs of basalt started out as lava that was released into the water when two tectonic plates pulled apart about 60 million years ago. The mass of lava started to cool almost instantly, but its whole surface didn't actually cool at the same rate. The lava that cooled the slowest formed the biggest of the columns, and the lava that cooled quickest formed the smallest columns.

The second kind of volcanic landforms are called intrusive. Intrusive land develops when magma gets stuck in the crust on its way to the surface and hardens. One type of intrusive landform is called a batholith. It's usually made of granite that's formed in the crust. Over time erosion brings it to the surface. Batholiths make up the core of some mountain ranges. The Sierra Nevada mountains in California are all giant batholiths.

Another kind of intrusive landform is called a laccolith. Laccoliths develop when magma rises through a conduit, pushing up the earth and rock

THE EXTRUSIVE LAVA COLUMNS OF GIANT'S CAUSEWAY

MOUNT HUMPHREYS' SUMMIT SPIRE IN THE SIERRA NEVADA MOUNTAINS

MISSOURI BATHOLITHS

ARIANNA SOLDATI

ONE REASON I LOVE GEOLOGY SO MUCH is that it is science that helps me understand the world around me. On road trips out West in the United States, I see these incredible rock formations. And as a geologist, I start making connections: Oh, that one is from an orogenic (mountain-building) event I studied. Or I realize that I'm looking at a landslide site. If you've got trained eyes, you can see where rock detached from the side of a hill or a mountain and where it accumulated farther downslope. Even when I'm on an airplane and look down from the window, I can recognize certain features. For example, the Finger Lakes in New York State were left behind by retracting glaciers about 10,000 years ago. Their elongated shape and parallel arrangement are clues to their formation.

I got my Ph.D. in Missouri. One of my favorite places to visit when I lived there was Elephant Rock State Park. Here there are intrusions called batholiths. These batholiths are gigantic: They look like enormous boulders that were just dropped down into the landscape from outer space. But they're really part of the feeding system for a long-extinct volcano. (A feeding system is what volcanologists call a volcano's complex magma chambers and conduits.) We don't really know how many chambers or conduits there are in a feeding system, or how they're arranged. We just know that somehow magma travels through them from the source. Only about 10 percent of the magma produced on Earth makes it out to the surface. The other 90 percent remains underground and solidifies. There are different reasons for this. Sometimes the magma cools down too much and can't move anymore. Or maybe it doesn't have enough gas in it to make it move very far in the first place. It's also possible there isn't enough magma in the chamber for an eruption to start. Whatever the reason, magma solidifies wherever it is. As thousands of years go by, the land on the surface around it erodes, and these intrusions become the only things that stand out in the landscape.

The batholiths at Elephant Rock State Park are a popular rock-climbing spot. They're also really pink, so they're interesting to look at!

ARIANNA TOOK THESE PHOTOS OF BATHOLITHS AT ELEPHANT ROCK STATE PARK.

THERE'S A LOT OF PINK GRANITE STREWN ALL OVER THE PARK.

ONE OF A KIND: SHIPROCK,
REMAINS OF A VOLCANIC NECK

LAVA SPIKES AT PINNACLES
NATIONAL PARK

above it to form a mushroom-shaped dome. Laccoliths harden underground, too, and also get exposed through erosion. They're not big enough to form mountains, though. Some of them are what we call buttes, hills with flat tops. Many of these can be seen across the U.S. states of Montana and Colorado.

There are a number of other kinds of intrusive landforms. It turns out, magma can make itself into all different kinds of shapes, like saucers (lopoliths), waves (phacoliths), and sheets (sills and dikes). But some of the landforms you can see as you travel the world are anomalies—that is, they're not quite like any other thing. One example is Shiprock. This 1,500-foot (457-m)-tall rock juts out of the desert in New Mexico. It's the remains of magma that hardened in the volcano's vent. This formation is also called a volcanic neck. When the volcano became extinct and slowly began to wear away, this tall, craggy structure is all that was left.

All of the rock structures you'll find inside Pinnacles National Park in California were caused by volcanic activity, too. But each type of structure formed at different times and in different ways. One of the park's most striking volcanic features is the 100-foot (30.5-m) lava spikes. The scientific name for these spikes is fossil fumaroles. They formed just before Mount Mazama collapsed 7,700 years ago. Mount Mazama had been erupting a lava made of pumice, which was quickly covered up by avalanches made of heavier rocks. Meanwhile, vents beneath the surface spewed hot gases, and these shaped the trapped pumice into cement-hard, and often hollow, spikes. They kind of look like sandcastles dribbled from wet sand by giants.

We know a lot about volcanoes, but there is still so much to be learned about the amazing volcanoes that have created our world. Who will make the next important discovery? Will it be you?

GET IN THE FLOW!

THIS EXPERIMENT CREATES A GIANT ERUPTION, so we suggest conducting it outside to make cleanup a snap. For maximum impact, decorate the cola bottle to look like a volcano!

DIY VOLCANIC ERUPTION

For this activity you'll need:

INDEX CARD

GOGGLES

2-LITER BOTTLE OF DIET COLA

(REGULAR COLA WILL WORK, TOO, BUT THE SUGAR IN REGULAR COLA LIMITS THE STRENGTH OF THE ERUPTION).

SCISSORS

1 ROLL OF MENTOS MINTS

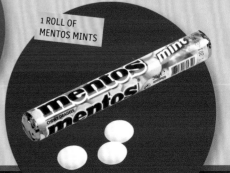

What to do:

1. Cut the index card into a circle and curl it up to form a funnel. You'll use the funnel to pour a bunch of Mentos into the cola bottle all at the same time.

2. Open the bottle of cola and the package of Mentos.

3. Place the bottle on a flat, sturdy surface. Doing this outside is best.

4. Put on the goggles, to protect your eyes.

5. Put the funnel on the mouth of the soda bottle and pour five Mentos into it at the same time.

6. Remove the funnel and back away from the bottle.

ERUPTION!

THE CANDY ACTS TO SPEED UP THE FIZZ POWER OF THE SODA, WHICH THEN CAUSES THE ERUPTION.

TRY THE EXPERIMENT WITH OTHER BOTTLES OF COLA AND VARY THE NUMBER OF MENTOS TO COMPARE THE HEIGHT AND DURATION OF THE ERUPTION.

FOR MORE VOLCANO READING, CHECK OUT:

Fradin, Dennis, and Judith. *Volcano! The Icelandic Eruption of 2010 and Other Hot, Smoky, Fierce, and Fiery Mountains.* Washington, DC: National Geographic, 2010.

Furgang, Kathy. *National Geographic Kids Everything Volcanoes and Earthquakes: Earthshaking Photos, Facts, and Fun!* Washington, DC: National Geographic, 2013.

Galat, Joan Marie. *National Geographic Readers: Erupt! 100 Fun Facts About Volcanoes.* Washington, DC: National Geographic, 2017.

Honovich, Nancy. *Ultimate Explorer Field Guide: Rocks and Minerals.* Washington, DC: National Geographic, 2016.

Peter, Carsten. *Extreme Planet: Carsten Peter's Adventures in Volcanoes, Caves, Canyons, Deserts, and Beyond!* Washington, DC: National Geographic, 2015.

Schreiber, Anne. *National Geographic Readers: Volcanoes!* Washington, DC: National Geographic, 2011.

AT THE SUMMIT OF PITON DE LA FOURNAISE ON RÉUNION ISLAND, ARIANNA LOOKS DOWN ON THE CLOUDS.

ARIANNA STANDING ACROSS A FRACTURE AT PITON DE LA FOURNAISE ON RÉUNION ISLAND

ARIANNA SITTING ON A LAVA BOMB AT CHAÎNE DES PUYS IN FRANCE

INDEX

Boldface indicates illustrations.

CREDITS

To the next generation of volcano explorers. —AS

For Ada, who's always loved a big, loud explosion. —LN

For more information, visit nationalgeographic.com, call 1-800-647-5463, or write to the following address:

National Geographic Partners
1145 17th Street N.W.
Washington, D.C. 20036-4688 U.S.A.

Visit us online at nationalgeographic.com/books

For librarians and teachers: ngchildrensbooks.org

More for kids from National Geographic: natgeokids.com

For information about special discounts for bulk purchases, please contact National Geographic Books Special Sales: specialsales@natgeo.com

For rights or permissions inquiries, please contact National Geographic Books Subsidiary Rights: bookrights@natgeo.com

Designed by Girl Friday Productions

Hardcover ISBN: 978-1-4263-3142-8
Reinforced library binding ISBN: 978-1-4263- 3143-5

ACKNOWLEDGMENTS
A heartfelt thank-you to my parents, partner, and friends for always supporting me as a volcano enthusiast; to National Geographic for inspiring me as a volcano explorer; and to my Ph.D. advisor for guiding me as a volcano scientist. —AS

Huge thanks to Girl Friday Productions and National Geographic for bringing me aboard this fun and fascinating project. —LN

The authors and publisher also wish to thank the book team: Shelby Lees, project editor; Kathryn Williams, editorial assistant; Amanda Larsen, art director; Sarah J. Mock, photo editor; Joan Gossett, production editor; and Anne LeongSon and Gus Tello, production assistants.

Printed in China
18/RRDS/1